To:

Hope you enjoy!

Tiger on a String

Kassie Overend

God bless you

Lots of love

Janet-Lea

This revised edition published by

LADRINGLOS PUBLICATIONS

24 Royd Mount, Rotcher Road,
Holmfirth, HD9 2QZ
2018

First published by
United Writers Publications
Trevail Mill - Zenner – St. Ives, Cornwall – 1977
ISBN 901976 42 3

All rights reserved. No part of this publication may be reproduced, stored in a retrieval system or transmitted, in any form or by any means, electronic, mechanical, photocopying, recording or otherwise without the prior permission of the copyright owner.

ISBN   978 1 5272 1752 2

Copyright © 1977 The Estate of Kassie Overend
All photographs © 1977 The Estate of
Kassie Overend

Printed by Book Printing UK
Remus House, Coltsfoot Drive,
Peterborough, PE2 9BF

Dedications, Acknowledgements and Thanks

This book is dedicated to the memory of my father, Wilfrid Overend and to my mother and sister Meg who together with myself, formed an acrobatic troupe known as the Ladringlos, and who later became Fenella's family.

To my cousin Elizabeth Edwards of Bournemouth, (free-lance writer) without whose advice and encouragement this book might not have been written and also to my brother-in-law, Dexter Ellis, for his helpful assistance and for reminding me of some events which I had forgotten.

Kassie Overend 1977

Foreword

My mother, Kassie Overend and the family had always lived in Holmfirth, Yorkshire and it was here in the 1920's that my grandparents formed their acrobatic act, The Ladringlos - which Kassie and her sister Meg joined as young teenagers.

In 1939 the family act received a contract to join Boswell's Circus in South Africa. Living in a moving train and travelling from place to place in a strange country was exciting.

The Ladringlos had been with the circus for six months when Mr. Boswell asked Kassie and Meg to look after two tiger cubs, snatched from their cannibalistic mother. Their joy was short-lived when one of these tiny creatures died, but the other, which they named Fenella, thrived. They all moved back to Holmfirth and Fenella lived with them as one of the family for 10 ½ years until her death in 1950.

Kassie and Meg then returned to performing their act as the Ladringlos until Meg was forced to retire due to ill health.

My mother continued to live in Holmfirth and died in 2014 aged 99.

Rosamund Dailly 2018

CONTENTS

Chapter		Page
1.	Circus Life in South Africa	1
2.	Nursemaids to Cubs	22
3.	Fenella – the Cub	31
4.	Return Voyage	52
5.	Fenella - in Quarantine	69
6.	Quarantine Continued	82
7.	Freedom	96
8.	We take Fenella to Blackpool	110
9.	Trouble with the Council	125
10.	Fenella - In 'Show Business'	142
11.	What, No Gun?	172
12.	On Tour	200
13.	The Curtain Falls	220

1

Circus Life in South Africa

Never in my wildest dreams had I ever thought I should become the owner of a tigress. I had always thought of tigers as ferocious animals behind bars in zoos, snarling and growling. In circuses, too, I had watched trainers, cracking their whips in the air, whilst lions and tigers, baring their teeth, unwillingly jumped from one high stool to another.

Sometimes I used to admire stage and screen personalities who were nursing lion cubs while posing for publicity photographs. Then I had wished I could have my photograph taken holding a lion cub, but that was as far as the dream went. However, fate had other plans, and this is how it happened.

I, along with my father, mother and sister, had performed with circuses and variety shows in an aerial act and had travelled practically throughout Britain.

The Ladringlos: Mr. and Mrs. Overend,
Kassie & Meg

One day, in April 1939, we were approached by an agent who asked if we were interested in a season with Boswell Brothers' Circus in South Africa. Of course we were. Cables went backwards and forwards; passports were obtained with amazing speed. There was great excitement and much rushing about; and in the short space of a week we were on our way crossing the Bay of Biscay on the R.M.S. Windsor Castle, resting and recovering, and hardly able to believe we had packed up and left home so quickly.

My sister's fortune for that year had read: "This will be the most exciting year of your life." We had laughed and joked about it but it began to look as though the prediction could be true, for here we were sailing into an unknown adventure.

On board the ship we met the Lindners, German artistes, consisting of two men and their wives. They had three lively young children, who delighted everyone by bobbing curtseys in true Nordic fashion, as they bade them "Guten Morgen".

The Lindners, like most German acrobats, were extremely conscientious and dedicated to their work. On the second day at sea, they fixed their perch and trapeze and began to practice their act. Every day, even when the ship rolled at dangerous angles in a heavy swell, Mr. Lindner would stand four square with the slender perch balanced on his shoulder, his eyes fixed on the top, while Conrad, his partner, climbed aloft and performed amazing feats, to the amusement of some passengers and consternation of others.

The voyage was most interesting, with the usual round of games, parties, dances and a visit to Madeira. The time raced by and in fourteen days we found ourselves at Cape Town, in a land of sunshine, blue skies and intense heat.

It is surprising how a sudden silence can affect one as much as a sudden noise, and on the last morning I was awakened by the cessation and complete silence of the ship's engines. I leapt from my berth, rushed to the port-hole excitedly, and with delight saw that the ship was now lying in Table Bay awaiting the pilot.

In the clear intensity of the early morning light the first sight of Table Mountain, rising like a great wall in majestic grandeur, spread with its table cloth of white clouds and flanked on the left by Devil's Peak, and on the right by the Lion's Head and Signal Hill, is a never to be forgotten sight. Its skyline looked almost as it must have done in 1652 when the three ships from the Dutch East India Company, the 'Dromedaris', the 'Goede Hoop' and the 'Reiger', manned by over a hundred men, dropped anchor in Table Bay. Under the command of Johan Van Riebeeck the first settlement was founded which later became known as Cape Town.

The morning was still and blue, and a curious aromatic scent of trees, herbs, harbours and heat, wafted gently from the land.

Our home in England was in the West Riding of Yorkshire, and the transition from the cold, bleak Pennine Hills and austere stone-work in walls and buildings was quite startling. In England it was spring, with the trees bursting into their fresh green foliage and the nearby woods a haze of bluebells. Here, on the south of the equator, where the seasons are reversed, the summer was already over. In Cape Town the shops were already displaying their winter clothes and furs. This seemed to us very strange as the weather was so warm. We were amazed at the low price of fruit in the shops; bananas were twenty for three-pence, and luscious, velvety grapes were twopence per pound.

Having a little time to spare before starting on the next leg of the journey to join the circus, my sister Meg and I wandered through the town and climbed the slopes of Signal Hill or the Lion's Rump as it is also known. From the hillside there was a magnificent view of the bay and adjoining mountains and we seated ourselves on some warm stones under the fragrant pines, to contemplate the view. The panorama was really exquisite and everywhere seemed so peaceful and beautiful on that hot, sunny afternoon.

A native workman suddenly appeared from nowhere and walked towards us. He looked anxious and I began to wonder if perhaps we were trespassing.

"Missi," he said, "not to sit there, very bad." We jumped up quickly in alarm. "Very bad," he repeated. "Scorpions, they live under stones, sting, bad, kill!" And so we learned that there were 'serpents' in our bit of Eden!

That evening found us on the 'Cape to Johannesburg' train to join the Boswell Circus, which was performing near Johannesburg. The journey lasted two nights and one day, and covered a distance of 956 miles. We began to realise the vastness of this country through which we were travelling. The grass and shrubs were dry and yellow, and we saw many 'koppies' or small hills on the horizon. A dusty red road ran alongside the railway track. On we went, travelling through many tiny villages or 'dorps'.

The tiny stations all looked alike, with low platforms, behind which were gum trees and dark, spiky conifers. Seats and waiting rooms were clearly marked - for black or white only - as even in 1939 there was strict segregation between the races.

We little realised at the time that those stations were to be a major part of our lives for the next twelve months and that together with the train they were to be, in fact, our home.

One of the most noticeable changes was the absence of the pleasant spring evenings we had left behind. The sun set at about five-thirty p.m. and darkness fell rapidly without any twilight. The sun disappeared behind the horizon and the sky became pale green. Stars twinkled brilliantly, whilst the hills changed from blue to deep purple as the train continued its long journey over the lonely veldt (grass country with few trees). Owls suddenly appeared and perched on the posts of the wire fencing at the side of the line.

During our first day on the train a telegram was delivered to us at one of the stations telling us to alight at Roodpoort, a small town ten miles before Johannesburg.

We arrived there at seven a.m. the next day and were met by Stanley Boswell, a tall, handsome young man, and one of the Boswell sons.

In the station buffet he regaled us with coffee and the most enormous sausage rolls I have ever seen. I should think they must have measured about three by seven inches. He told us that the circus train would be coming through before long and would pick us all up. We waited in eager anticipation for what seemed like hours and I wondered what the train would look like. Would it have brightly painted carriages with the name of the circus written across it as do the caravans of tenting circuses? Time dragged on and we waited - it grew hotter and hotter.

Waiting for the train

The Lindner children played hopscotch on the dusty, deserted platform, but they soon grew bored. After a while Janni, the youngest child, hot and weary, ran up to her mother and leaned against her. "Mutti", she said in a plaintive voice, "I'm tired, I want to go home." Her mother picked up her little one, took her on her knee and consoled her, "But, liebchen, your home is where your mutti is."

Suddenly a bell clanged, the train was approaching, and there was a shimmering, in the distance, like a small mirage. Almost silently it glided along the railway line.

At first it looked like an ordinary train, two long brown coaches with the letters S.A.R. written several times in large letters, and the South African emblem of the springbok imprinted on the glass windows. A line of trucks followed; some were open whilst others were closed in and, of course, there was an engine at the front and a guard's van at the rear. Later I learned that this rear van was called a 'caboose' and the driver and his mate lived in it whilst making their long journeys through South Africa. I soon found out, however, that it was very different from an ordinary train. On top of the open trucks were a variety of wagons painted in bright colours, emblazoned with the words: BOSWELL BROTHERS CIRCUS, and filled with all the paraphernalia of a travelling show.

There were trucks with lions and tigers, elephants, camels, horses and monkeys, tenting and seating, props, tractors and cars. The trucks seemed endless and the noise was deafening. Thankfully, we clambered aboard.

Along the corridor came the pungent smell of fried onions and garlic, and further on again we could hear quick staccato voices and snatches of a flamenco song which seemed to quiver in the air. Mrs. Boswell welcomed us with cups of tea and at last we felt we had arrived!

The Circus Train

During the early hours of the morning the train had pulled out of the siding where we stayed the night and travelled on some thirty miles to a sleepy little 'dorp' or village amongst blue gum trees. The scene was one of bustle and excitement as the activities of our first day with Boswell's Circus began.

The trucks and coaches (in which we lived and slept) were separated, and the latter were put out of the way on the deserted side-line. The trucks (containing the animals and equipment) were shunted to an off-loading platform, and their iron sides clanked down to rest on the main platform. Tractors then carefully eased the wagons with their heavy loads on to the platform, after which they were taken by tractor to the circus site.

That first morning the site was close to the railway track, making the operation comparatively easy. On many occasions, however, the town would be several miles from the railway and each tractor would have to make the journey two or three times, bouncing and bumping over the uneven, dusty roads.

Often the first thing to be done would be to burn the small, scrub-like plants in the area to make it smooth for the circus ring. Then the tent was erected by a gang of native tent boys under the supervision of a white tent master. They would chant in unison as they hauled away on the ropes of the vast tent and always seemed a happy-go-lucky crowd.

The elephants and camels would be unloaded and taken on the veldt with their respective keepers - the camels bucking and cantering - to graze and laze until the time of their performance.

Elephants outside the circus tent

We wandered across the dusty, sandy square into the one and only general store there seemed to be, and were made welcome by the storekeeper. He was delighted when he learned we had recently left England. "I'm from Wales." he said. He invited us to have coffee and treated us like long-lost relations.

Living in a train was quite an experience, and totally

different from dwelling in a house. Often we found our cramped quarters rather trying and wished for a little more comfort. Still, we got used to it.

The train was hired from the South African State Railways at considerable cost, and included the services of the driver and the mate. One of the two connecting coaches was for the Boswells, their family and staff, and the other for the artistes.

We (the four of us) were allocated one compartment and a coupé (that is, half a compartment). Unlike a caravan which has built-in cupboards and other facilities, these were the second-class sleeping coaches used on long overnight journeys. The seating was of green leather and there were upper bunks at either side. There was a wash-basin between the windows, over which was a narrow folding-up table. This could be pushed up against the wall when not in use.

Each family was responsible for their own cooking, so one of our first purchases was an oil stove, small oven, pots, pans and various other equipment.

During the day the compartment could be overbearingly hot, whilst at night we froze. Life was far more primitive here than we had expected. Apparently, in American circuses, a cookhouse is provided and the artistes are well looked after.

But life, as usual, has its compensations, for here we were, travelling high above the grit and dust of the railroad and every day, as we journeyed from place to place, the panoramic scenery of South Africa unfolded before us. To see all this from a train window, or from the observation platform at the end of the coach, with no worries of traffic or driving and a compartment of one's own, must surely be the ideal way of seeing so large a country.
We would gaze with awe at the grandeur of the scenery, the train groaning as it climbed up mountainsides, looping one way and another. Sometimes it was necessary to have an engine pulling in front and another pushing behind, to get us over the precipitous heights.

Sometimes the gradient would be too steep for the train and it would have to be divided. The front half would be taken up by the engine, then it would return for the other half. At other times we would travel over immense tracts of veldt, leaving the main line and travelling up single branch lines to the railhead, performing at each small village or 'dorp' along the route.

Africa is full of branch lines which come to an abrupt end meaning we would have to travel all the way back again to the main line, after which we could proceed to the next place.

Usually these long journeys took place on a Sunday and lasted all day. This was regarded as our day of rest from the circus, no fixing up of apparatus, no practising or rehearsing.

During the journey, artistes visited each other's compartments to talk or play cards. There was a halt for lunch, also to feed the animals and take on water. Sometimes, when the gradient was very steep and the train was slowly puffing and chugging in short bursts of energy and steam to keep moving, we would jump off. Running alongside, we would gather mimosa and gourds which grew in abundance by the side of the railway.

Hitching a lift on a circus truck going to town

Along many of these lines there was often only one train per week, so a travelling circus was an outstanding event for everyone. The farms, for miles around, would have been previously informed of the circus's arrival by postal advertisements. Gradually, during the afternoon, farmers, with their wives, families and workers, would arrive from all directions in wagons, lorries, Cape carts, or on horseback. Native husbands, accompanied by their wives, whose babies were strapped to their backs, and wide-eyed children, would trek in from outlying districts. With many travelling circuses, the artistes are expected to help in various ways besides performing and we were soon asked to assist at the front of the tent. We had to show people to their seats and to pack them in when there was a full house. It was fascinating to observe the different types and races who came to the show.

Some natives strolled in majestically, wearing their brightly coloured blankets and smoking pipes, whilst others who had bought tickets stood outside, shaking with nervousness and too afraid to come in. Eventually, plucking up courage, they entered timidly through the canvas awning and into a world of wonder, their eyes rolling as they came into the brilliantly lit tent. Quickly they used to scuttle along to the native gallery where part of the seating was partitioned for them.

The amount of seating allotted to the natives and the whites varied in different parts of the country. On the Rand, in the gold mining communities, there was only a small portion for the white people as the population consisted mainly of coloured miners. In Natal, however, where there were many Indians, there was a special gallery for them as well, as they would not mix with the natives. Consequently, because of the different languages and races there were no programmes printed.

The Indians arrived with enormous families, all of whom had to be sorted out. Sometimes it was most complicated as the youngest ones came in free. We had to count and recount them in case they had tucked an extra couple of children under the mother's sari.

The father used to come through the tent flap first clutching a fist full of tickets, followed by his wife, who usually wore a sari and had a red caste mark on her forehead. After them would be a flotilla of children of all sizes, with dark, enquiring eyes.

Carefully we used to count the tickets, perhaps ten of them, then the children, " Twelve, thirteen - no fourteen! Are you sure?" Then we started again and counted them for the second time. Finally we used to give it up - oh, well, what's the odd one or two? But by that time they had swept excitedly by us and were already sitting upon the high seating, mixed with all the others and, to me, all looking alike.

The entrance to the tent was a great place from which to spot and collect native ornaments. When a native appeared wearing some interesting beadwork or carrying an unusual knob kerry (a stick with a large knob), Conrad (of the Lindners), who was good at negotiating, would take him to one side. A little bargaining took place and then the native trotted to his seat with a broad grin and a few shillings the richer, whilst one of us would be the possessor of yet another trophy.

Many natives arrived penniless and were unable to afford the entrance fee but they were happy to stand outside and watch proceedings.

The huge tent glowed like an illuminated balloon. Electric lights festooned the entrance, around which a thousand night-flying insects danced as in exhilaration. Artistes and grotesquely painted clowns in vivid costumes passed constantly between the dressing tent and ring door. Lions roared and elephants trumpeted, raising their ever-enquiring trunks.

The natives stood and gazed, fascinated, swaying to the music and shuffling their bare feet. There was so much to see and such excitement, colour and noise, even if they could not go inside to watch the show. When the performance was finished they were still unable to leave this scene of animation and would light camp fires under the gum trees, then stay overnight, wrapped in their blankets to protect them from the intense cold of the night air. All this time they were laughing and singing together.

That year too, Meg and I did something we had always longed to do - we became part of a riding act. Although the circus had an extensive programme, including three trapeze acts, ladder balancers, jugglers, two wire acts, equilibrists, performing sea-lions, monkeys, camels, lions, elephants and innumerable horses, there was no riding act. Now a riding act is an integral part of a circus, without which no show is complete. The circus proprietors were well aware of this fact, as the Dutch farmers, who lived on isolated farms on the veldt, used to approach them regularly and enquire expectantly: "Have you any lady riders with you this year?"

Therefore, almost as soon as we arrived, Meg and I were asked if we would be interested in forming a riding act along with another artiste. That we were thrilled is to put it mildly, and although we had never done any riding before we agreed immediately. Rehearsals began at once and in less than seven weeks the vaultage act was included in the show. Although it was a comparatively simple act, it served the purpose and the circus owners could proudly proclaim that they now had lady riders performing in the ring!

The atmosphere in the big top was often unbearably hot and we felt this particularly during our trapeze act as we swung and spun high in the dome of the tent. The blazing sun beat down on the canvas and our hands perspired so much that if we hadn't put large quantities of powdered resin on them we could easily have slipped and fallen to the ground.

**Mr. W. Boswell, Kassie, Meg & Doreen.
Riding lesson**

Every day brought the same routine; yet every day was different. We never knew where we were going or what the next place would be like. Incidents occurred, acts left, new acts came, animals died, new ones arrived. Some days we were sweltering in sizzling heat; on other days violent storms almost blew the tent down. Occasionally we arrived late in a town and there was a mad scramble to get the tent up in time for the evening's show, but up it went and the show went on; always the show went on!

That was the pattern of our life for six months; until the morning that one of the Boswell brothers came to our compartment and said to my sister and me: "How would you like to be nursemaids to two tiger cubs?"

Thus came about our first introduction to what was to be almost eleven years' association with Fenella, who later became known as:

"FENELLA, the DOMESTICATED TIGER."

2

Nursemaids to Cubs

Some places, perhaps because of their association with a special event, remain in one's mind forever. Such a place was White River, a small subtropical town surrounded by rolling hills in south-east Transvaal and near the gateway to the Kruger National Park. We had by now travelled extensively through the Transvaal, Natal, Orange Free State, Basutuland, and on the morning of September 6th, 1939, three days after Britain declared war on Germany, we arrived at White River.

This was the morning when Mr. Boswell interrupted our breakfast with his startling request. Meg and I were thrilled at the idea of looking after two tiger cubs and little thought of what this would involve. Eagerly, we jumped up and followed him quickly out of the train, along the railway tracks, past numerous trucks in which were cages containing lions, monkeys, sea-lions, and a pair of adult tigers, until we arrived at an empty truck.

Swinging ourselves up on to this, we noticed a big, untidy pile of sacking being carefully guarded by a solemn-faced native boy. With the air of a magician about to perform an amazing illusion trick, Mr. Boswell deftly removed the sacking. We could hardly believe our eyes. There, underneath the sacking, lay two newly-born tiger cubs. They were still wet and bedraggled with sawdust and smelly filth sticking to their woolly fur. The native keeper of the menagerie (for there was a menagerie in addition to the circus), had raked them out from under the bars of the cage in which they had just been born, knowing that on previous occasions the mother tiger had immediately killed her young.

We gazed, fascinated. "They're striped!" I suddenly said in amazement. Meg gave me a condescending look. "Of course, silly, tigers are striped, you know." Somewhat crushed, I replied, "Yes, but I thought they would be plain first, and then become striped later."

Carefully, we carried them back to our compartment in the circus train. They mewed pitifully as we began to clean them, their eyes tightly closed; they seemed pathetic things and very weak as they wobbled blindly about.

My mother stroked each one with a finger. "Poor little mites, they're so tiny," she said, but I could see she was also wondering where we could keep them with such small floor space.

However, Meg and I were jubilant. Tiger Cubs! This was the most marvellous happening since our arrival in Africa. Their buff-coloured fur was woolly, with distinctive and prominent black stripes. Their short, black and buff tails were closely striped. They had tiny, almost invisible ears which were white inside and black with a white spot outside.

Their whiskers were pale and silky and already their tiny claws were needle sharp. They were only fifteen inches long and their flat, patterned faces gave them the appearance of two small, wizened owls. We put them in a box and wrapped them in woollies. Mr. Boswell, always resourceful, produced from somewhere a baby's feeding bottle and sent out for a tin of full-cream dried milk powder.

We were very anxious at first whether they would accept milk from us, but this proved to be no problem. While Meg nursed one, I gently put the teat into its crying mouth and squeezed a few drops of milk on to its tiny pink tongue; then we repeated this with the other one and soon they were both taking milk without any trouble. We would feed them about every two hours but they seemed so unsettled and cried nearly all the time.

"Don't expect them to live," Mr. Boswell had warned us "Tiger cubs are very delicate and extremely difficult to rear."

Fenella ten days old - her first outing

Sadly, I began to think that this was to be the case, for they cried practically incessantly, day and night. Did I say cry? It was a high, piercing wail, and became most nerve wracking. As soon as one quietened down, the other would begin, and as the train travelled on through the night and early morning, we were wakened again and again from sleep to heat the milk on the oil stove, and to feed first one and then the other. Sometimes I thought I could have strangled them, but instead my sister and I would patiently nurse them, always trying to comfort and console them.

Although the days were hot, the nights were cold and frosty - there was even a violent snow storm one night - so we had to keep them well wrapped up in soft, warm woollies during the night. Then, one morning, to our dismay, when they were both ten days old, one of them, for no apparent reason, appeared much weaker and refused the milk.

In vain we tried to save its life. Mr. Boswell gave it brandy and Meg nursed it continually, keeping it warm, but it was of no avail and in the afternoon it died.

In the midst of the trouble and confusion Mr. Wallenda, the sea-lion trainer, walked in, bringing with him a strong aroma of fish, and in order to cheer us up he suggested that we should have the skin cured. His boy, Mafuto, was "quite good at that sort of thing," he said. Miserably, we agreed and off he went, carrying with him the limp little body. Shortly afterwards he returned with the pelt, but on being confronted with the raw skin, poor Meg, who such a short time before had been nursing the cub, was so shocked that she burst into tears and was inconsolable for a long time.

I, too, was upset and deeply disappointed by its death, for even though the two cubs had been a handful, I had become very fond of them both and dearly hoped we should be able to rear the pair. I was worried too in case the remaining one should suddenly die. But to our surprise and pleasure, this cub became more settled, and slept much better as it was no longer disturbed by the wailing and crying of the other one. She (by now we knew she was a baby tigress) was an endearing little thing and Meg and I nursed her most of the day. This she enjoyed, much preferring it to being left on her own in her box.

Cub on the bottle

After a fortnight her eyes began to open, bluish and filmy, and she tried, feebly, to struggle and clamber out of the box.

She was always ready for her bottle, and when suckling would use a kneading action with her paws, flexing her sharp little claws in and out like a domestic cat. This was bliss for her, but not very comfortable for the person nursing her. I always put a thick rug over my legs to prevent her claws from giving me innumerable tiny scratches.

Just as we thought all our troubles were over, to my dismay, she, too, began to be ill. From the beginning she had had a tendency to constipation, which became more pronounced and then was accompanied by sickness. We were frantic with worry and I wondered miserably if our second cub was going to die.

We were working in Kimberley at the time. In desperation I rushed into the town and fortunately found a helpful chemist, who suggested that I try liquid paraffin in her milk. I hurried back to take his advice and gave her a little with her next feed; to our relief this put matters right. Then, quite by accident, I found out something about tiger cubs which, I suppose, is the same with all members of the cat family. I was feeding her, and at the same time cleaning her side and back legs with a cloth wrung out in warm water, as her fur had become sticky with milk, when without any effort at all she began to excrete. It was then I discovered one of the facts of life, which every tiger mother knows by instinct that a baby cub can't function naturally unless stimulated by its mother's rough tongue, or something similar. We were, I must admit, very ignorant nursemaids.

When it seemed probable that she would live, we decided to give her a name. Up to then it had been, "The Tiger" or "The Cub", and as we had come from Yorkshire, sometimes we would say in fun, "Now then John Willie" and "Come on Henry James". Everyone suggested names: Ranee, Cleo, Selina, were all considered and tossed aside. Names of aunts and cousins - Mabel, Maud, Agnes - were mulled over and discarded. However, I happened to be reading a most interesting story in Tit Bits in which the heroine's name was Fenella. The name appealed to me, and we all repeated it aloud several times – Fenella, Fenella - and all agreed that it had a really feline sound to it. Yes, most suitable for a tigress, so Fenella she became.

A few weeks after this, Mr. Boswell came to our compartment again, to ask us this time if we would look after two lion cubs for the day while their parents were being put into separate cages. These cubs, too, had just escaped from being eaten by their cannibalistic father by the timely action of the animal keeper who, as in the case of the tiger cubs, had raked them out of the cage. The other two cubs of this litter had not been so fortunate and had already been devoured.

We noted with interest that from the first day they were bigger and stronger than the tiger cubs had been, and even at that tender age were able to struggle and climb out of their box; they took readily and eagerly to the bottle.

Fenella was afraid of these lusty youngsters and, as they groped blindly about the floor, she spat and hit out at them with her tiny paw and then, in disgust, toddled off into the coupé next door, where my mother picked her up and nursed her.

In the evening, when the show was over and the audience shuffled slowly out of the tent, Meg and I stood at the exit, holding the two lion cubs in our arms. With exclamations of "Oohs" and "Aahs", "Aren't they cute?" and "Aren't they cuddly?" people stroked and admired them. When the public had left, thankfully, we carried the cubs back to the menagerie where they were reunited with their anxious mother, and we returned to our compartment in the train, to make amends to our very dear Fenella.

3

Fenella - The Cub

Fenella was six weeks old when I tried supplementing her diet with mutton broth, which she drank from her bottle. She loved it from the start, taking it so greedily that a week later I gave her some cooked, minced mutton and the shank to gnaw on. With ever increasing interest she paced up and down the compartment, as soon as she smelled the rich, tantalising aroma of simmering soup and meat she mewed shrilly and impatiently at our slowness in serving the delicious food.

Not only did she like meat, but she enjoyed vegetable soup especially the carrots and onions. It was just as well we all enjoyed mutton stew, for having only the one oil stove to cook on, it was a case of - stew for one, stew for all.

Experimenting with other foods, as one does with a puppy or kitten I found she liked any kind of milky food, pudding and custard but sniffed disdainfully at cakes, biscuits, bread and chocolate - which she considered inedible. To my surprise she enjoyed home-made chips. I think she liked the fat they were cooked in, and she would even eat a fried egg occasionally. This was not exactly tiger diet, but Fenella thrived on it. An entry in my diary reads: "Cooked egg and chips for Fenella and myself this evening."

Fenella soon became a very clean creature and very regular in her habits, seeming to have an inborn desire, like a cat, not to foul her quarters. At first I made her a litter tray of newspaper but she quickly learned to wait for her early walk when, as soon as the train stopped, I hurriedly rushed her out onto the grass, Fenella soon realised the purpose of her early morning walk. There were a few 'misses' but under the circumstances who could blame her?

Fenella still could not see properly, and although by this time she could walk very well, she was always bumping into something: in fact, I used to think sadly that she was going to remain semi-blind. To assist her, my father made a little harness for Fenella of soft leather which he had originally purchased to make into acrobatic shoes. Fenella grew to rely on this harness for guidance and support, and it also made quite a good handle with which to pick her up.

I fastened a red silk dressing-gown cord to it for a lead, and when I went shopping Fenella accompanied me. She still followed more by sound than sight and often fell into hollows or stumbled over humps. When Fenella became tired, I would carry her in a flat-bottomed basket, a mode of travel which she loved.

Gradually, and to my delight, her sight improved. I noticed that if I wore white shoes she could follow me more easily. Sometimes, however, she lost herself in the long grass and her frightened howls were pitiful to hear.

Fenella with harness

Fenella gradually developed another noise, besides the mewing howls. This was a friendly, acknowledging sound to greet us and we called it chuckling. She did it by blowing down her nose in a quick succession and it sounded like " Hm Hm Hm Hm." On returning to the train after each show, Fenella always made a great fuss and greeted each one of us in turn, chuckling with pleasure and falling about limp and floppy with delight.

When we took Fenella for a walk, native children would call out "Look, there's a leopard!" As there are no wild tigers in South Africa, it was understandable that they should mistake her for the leopard, which is a native of South Africa.

I often went to look at Fen's parents who were a handsome pair of Sumatran tigers, and marvelled that our pudgy little dun and black cub would one day be a sleek-coated creature like her mother and father. Fenella's parents were on show in the menagerie and were housed in one of the red painted wagons which were taken daily back and forth to the circus tent. As they were not performers they spent their time pacing up and down, lean and slinky, awaiting their next meal of horse flesh.

Some days they would be lying indolent and bored, side by side, blinking their amber eyes and yawning - the male with his paw over the female in a protective manner. They always seemed very affectionate towards each other. I imagine they must have been born in a zoo and had never known what it was like to be free. The mother had always killed her cubs: possibly, deep down in her feline mind, she realised that a menagerie was no place for her children to be brought up.

Fenella at 8 weeks

As the weeks went by the weather became much hotter. The burning sun beat down on the railway carriages so that it became unbearably stifling inside. Fenella, or Fen as we often called her, found that the coolest place was under the carriage seat, and she used to spend the middle of the day there, stretched out as flat as a mat and panting in the heat.

The time flew by and soon it was Christmas in South Africa, and midsummer also. We arrived at Potchefstroom, the oldest town in the Transvaal, where we were actually to spend three whole days over the Christmas period. What a welcome change from the usual daily travelling! But it was a strange sort of Christmas, under the bluest of blue skies, in a sweltering heat of 90 degrees in the shade. Gardens everywhere were a blaze of colour with roses, marigolds, gladioli and the exotic tropical bougainvillea, cannas and hibiscus.

As there was an evening performance on Christmas day, the Boswells held a lunch-time party for all the circus members at one of the big hotels in the town. I suppose the Christmas tradition is the same the world over, for there was the usual turkey, plum pudding, mince pies, crackers and wine. Later, during the stifling heat of the afternoon, when the festivities were over, we drifted back to the railway station.

Those of us who were not overcome by heat, food and good South African wine began reminiscing of previous Christmases spent in totally different surroundings - of frost, deep snow, pantomimes and other circuses we had performed with, of our grandmothers at home in war-torn England. Suddenly, amidst all this blazing sunshine, I felt unaccountably homesick and wished that I too were back home.

Fenella 9 ½ weeks with Meg

Fenella, at three months, was a very lively and playful cub. To my relief her sight was perfect and she could almost outrun me. When awake she was hardly ever still; she stalked, hid, pounced, chewed, 'mouthed' on fingers, then ran off and hid behind a bush or even a leaf, thinking no doubt that as long as there was something to hide behind she wouldn't be seen. Sometimes, to tease her, my sister Meg and I would hide and Fenella, thinking she was lost, would stand and cry just like a child, then, when we suddenly jumped out from behind a bush, she was so happy to see us again that she was overcome with joy and rubbed against our legs, crying to be picked up.

Early every morning the train had to journey to a fresh place, there were bumps, bangs and backbreaking jolts as the trucks were shunted and pushed into position, therefore, from being a tiny cub, Fenella was used to noise, travel, change and a life full of events.

Three weeks after Christmas the circus moved down country to open at Wolseley in lovely Cape Province, and for the next month we toured the enchanting towns and villages amidst rugged, majestic mountains where in the valleys are huge fruit farms and vineyards. On the first day we were told we must not miss seeing the spectacular scenery as we travelled through Michells Pass on the way up to Ceres, which is ten miles from Wolseley, so, early the following morning, my mother - who was ever a light sleeper - awoke us, and shivering in the chill morning air we went out on to the observation platform.

Here indeed was a scene of grandeur. The wildness of the surroundings accentuated the height of these mighty mountains, their jagged peaks towering in the pale morning sky. The railroad which had been hewn out of the side of the mountains, perched, at times precariously, hundreds of feet above the dark, sinister and swirling River Breede below. Clutching their cameras, my father and another member of the show climbed daringly onto the coach roof to take cine films, shouting down to us to warn them if a tunnel was in sight as they had no wish to be decapitated as the train curved and wound upwards through the narrow pass. Ceres - known as the Switzerland of South Africa - is a most beautiful town at the summit of Michells Pass. Its wide streets are lined with oak trees, and it is surrounded by mountains which are snowcapped in winter.

Baboons live in the mountains and cause damage to the farmers' crops by coming down in troops to forage the orchards. I scanned the slopes eagerly, hoping to spot some of them but failed to see any. However, later that day when calling at a nearby farm to buy fruit, I was told by the farmer that only that morning he had shot a baboon which, with its family and friends, had been raiding his pear orchard. "It's just over here," he said, and I followed eagerly across the garden to a cluster of trees. Somehow I expected to see it lying on the ground but with a sense of shock, found he had strung its body, spread-eagled, upon a tree. Its dead face was so human-looking, just like a grotesque old man. I was aghast, I had very much wanted to see a baboon, but not like that. The farmer was obviously pleased with himself. "There," he said with great satisfaction, "that'll scare the others away!"

It was while we were at Ceres that I discovered yet another facet of Fenella's personality. Although she never seemed to object to getting wet, and often splashed happily through the irrigation channels at the sides of the streets, I had always thought that being of the cat family she would not like deep water. However, while I was paddling knee-deep in a cool tranquil pool in the upper reaches of the river, I heard little splashing sounds at my side and there, to my astonishment, swimming valiantly alongside me, was Fenella. I thought at first that she must have fallen in, but soon realised that this was not possible as the river was sandy and on a gentle slope. It was obvious therefore that she had deliberately walked in until she was out of her depth and had to swim. She wasn't enjoying it very much though and made little spitting sounds when the water lapped over her nose. Suddenly, appearing to see the far bank across the deep water, she began to swim towards it. Fortunately Fenella was wearing her harness, with the lead guide trailing behind on the water, so I was able to grab this and guide her back into the shallows. She scrambled out, bedraggled and rather surprised by this new achievement. She must have thought I was deserting her and so had bravely followed me.

The following week the circus visited Simonstown - the African naval base on the Coast of False Bay, with lovely rocky coves nearby and smooth beaches of pale sand. On an afternoon when there was no matinee, a crowd of us decided to spend the day at Seaforth, a pretty little spot, which reminded me of the bays around Guernsey.

As always, Fenella came too. She loved the beach and the shining sea, and frolicked and splashed in the small, warm waves on the fringe of the bay. Then she would hide and pounce at us from behind a fisherman's boat.

Later on, while I was swimming in the sea, Fenella - not to be outdone - followed me deeper and deeper into the water, appearing much more confident than the previous time. I put my hand under her chin, as one does with a learner, to lift her over the bigger waves and prevent the salt water from going into her mouth. All the time I talked and encouraged the new swimmer.

As we approached the shore Fenella noticed my mother who was chatting with Doreen, the clown's wife, whilst kneeling in the shallow water, swishing her hands backwards and forwards. With joyful recognition, Fenella bounded towards my mother and scrambled, slippery and wet, onto her shoulder and to everyone's amusement, succeeded in ducking her under the next wave.

Everywhere the family went, Fenella went too - whether it was visiting friends in their homes, picnics, or just shopping.

When there was a matinee - usually twice or three times a week - I tied her to the handle of our large theatrical hamper in the dressing tent before we went into the ring to give our act. There were always crowds of natives around the tent and they came to stand and gaze, fascinated by and yet scared of this strange jungle creature which lived in the circus as one of the family. They gathered together, talking excitedly in their native tongue, pointing and gesticulating, their big eyes rolling. Fenella - intrigued by their shining black legs and bare feet - strained and pulled on her lead to give chase, but we always managed to keep her at a safe distance.

It was not often practicable however to take Fenella to the evening show, with all the hustle and bustle of packing to be done afterwards, so poor Fenny had to be left behind in the train. Being left behind was the one thing that Fenella disliked most of all.

Meg and I had to leave particularly early as, besides being on duty at the entrance before the show, we were also in a riding act in the first part of the programme. My parents stayed behind with Fenella as long as possible, then they had to lock her up in our compartment and hurry along to the tent for our aerial act. The tigress's mournful cries followed them until they were out of earshot. On our return after the show, Fenella, overjoyed, made an enormous fuss of each of us in turn, before settling down for the night.

It soon became evident that Fenella knew us individually. One evening, Meg and I were invited to a party after the show. When we arrived back at the train in the early hours of the next morning, Fenella was pacing up and down our compartment. "I don't know what on earth is the matter with her," said my mother wearily. "She will not settle down and go to sleep. I feel sure she must be waiting for you to come home." At first we could not believe this, but my mother was right. Fenella greeted us both with effusive chuckles whilst we loved and cuddled her affectionately, then, quite contented, she ambled off into her box and was soon in a deep sleep.

In the train it was necessary for Fenella to be fastened up most of the time for her own safety, as she could easily have walked out along the corridor and jumped down onto the railway track. Usually I tied her lead to the leather window strap and she played happily at jumping on and off the carriage seat. Fenella was amazingly adept and seemed to know how far she could reach without becoming entangled. Although holes were chewed in blankets and cushions and sandals and bones were gnawed, she never attempted to chew the lead or bite the leather window strap.

A favourite game was to crouch down on the seat by the compartment door; when anyone walked along the corridor, Fenella swung out, putting all her weight on the lead, and gave them a smart cuff on the back as they passed. The circus children thought this was great fun and used to dash backwards and forwards encouraging Fenella to hit them, but there was one man who decided that Fenella should be taught a lesson. When she cuffed him with her paw he, in return, hit Fenella sharply on the nose. Fenella never forgave the man, and would spit quietly whenever she heard his footstep.

It was uncanny the way she recognised the man immediately from his light gait.

Water melons fascinated Fenella - the large, dark green variety, which I associate with wide-eyed, grinning piccaninnies. She played with one for hours, climbing on top of it, sprawling, falling off, and attempting to sink her tiny teeth into its hard, green skin. She also regarded corn cobs - known as 'mealies' in South Africa - as playthings, and loved to chase them and send them scattering along the floor.

During the night Fenella insisted on sleeping on my bed and grumbled and growled whenever I disturbed her by turning over. It was necessary to fasten her to the window strap at the foot as she used to wake early and then took a fancy to chewing my hair, she particularly liked to pull and chew at curlers. If Fenella became very restless I tucked her in bed with me where, after initial squirming and chewing my fingers, she fell asleep, lulled by the soporific movement of the train wheels and the warm contact with my body.

The Boswell Brothers often warned us that Fenella would turn wild, and in preparation for that day they had a cage all ready for her. When she was about four months old we thought this had actually happened.

That particular morning some friends of the Boswells visited them, and one of their sons came to ask me if he could borrow Fenella to show to these visitors. Feeling some-what apprehensive I agreed. Shortly afterwards I heard shouts and there was the son, running, panting and looking worried. "Miss Overend, Miss Overend," he cried breathlessly, "the tiger has turned wild! She's escaped and run away. Can you come quickly?"

My heart beat frantically as I raced along the train corridor. Was this the moment so often predicted, and if so what would happen to Fenella now? I jumped down on to the track and rushed along the line to a row of trucks where some of the Boswells and lots of other people were standing together, talking excitedly, as they peered under the trucks.

"She's under there," Mr. Boswell called out, "but whatever you do, don't go near her - she's gone completely wild; listen to the noise she's making."

Cautiously, I dropped down on to my knees and crept a little way under the truck. There was Fenella, crouched against a wheel, snarling, spitting and baring her teeth.

"Be careful." someone called out. "'You mustn't go any nearer. It's not safe - she'll attack you! "

I remained still and spoke very softly. "Fenny, Fenny, come Fenny." For a moment she stared, her amber eyes glittering and looking very bright in the shadow of her truck. Slowly I moved forward, hiding the fear in my heart and speaking softly all the time. Fenella remained motionless and taut, and to my pleasure allowed me to come near and to pick her up. Her little body suddenly became limp with relief as she felt my arms around her. With affection she rubbed her face against mine, chuckling all the time, almost as though she was saying: "Oh, it's so good to see you again. Why did you let me go away from you?"

Poor Fenella. She had panicked and become frightened at finding herself alone with a lot of strangers who were handling her in unfamiliar ways, she had clawed herself free and fled! Holding her carefully I carried her back to the train, and from the safety of my arms she turned and spat over my shoulder at everyone in that crowd. As for the young man who had carried her away, Fenella used to spit at him every time she saw him or heard his footsteps.

There was another occasion when I thought that the prediction of Fenella turning wild might be coming true. That particular day the circus was performing at the pretty town of Elgin. The tent had to be erected some distance from the train, which meant a long walk in the heat through an orchard, thick with luscious peaches, and then along a hillside lined with fir trees. I was walking through a wood; Fenella, on her lead, ambled along beside me, when I noticed suddenly that tiny red insects were creeping up my bare ankles. I shuddered, thinking they were red spiders, and hastily knocked them away, then forgot all about the incident.

**Meg with Fenella standing by
the circus train**

The following day, to our surprise, Fenella was extremely irritable and bad-tempered. She fidgeted, was restless, and snapped and snarled, baring her teeth. At first we thought she must be ill and then, becoming more anxious, we wondered if this was the beginning of 'wildness'.

Fenella glowered, stalked up and down, and lashed her tail furiously from side to side in a most unfriendly way. We were all mystified and could think of no reason for her strange behaviour. What a miserable and uncomfortable day it was!

I discovered the cause the following morning, when I suddenly spotted a small blue-black lump, about as big as a match head in the corner of Fenella's nostril. Then I saw another in the fold of her ear, then another, and another! She was full of them, under her fur, beneath her toes – everywhere! Feeling intensely shocked I realised they were ticks. They had buried themselves into Fenella's skin and bloated themselves on her blood.

The problem was, we couldn't get them out - their tenacity was amazing. As Meg and I pulled at them, the body broke leaving the head embedded and a nasty, squashy mess on our fingers. It was absolutely sickening. Someone suggested touching each tick with a lighted cigarette - an idea we turned down with horror, as it would cause so much suffering to Fenella. In any case her fur was too thick. Mother wondered if Flit spray would destroy the ticks. This seemed a better idea but again, Fenella's thick fur prevented effective results. Also, Fenella took an intense dislike to the spray, and quickly dived under the carriage seat from where she snapped angrily at us. Almost despairing, we tried drops of paraffin, and this proved to be the answer. A little paraffin dabbed carefully on each plump, gorged body, caused the creatures slowly to release their hold and drop to the floor. It required about three days to clear poor Fenella of all these obnoxious parasites, but perseverance was rewarded and to our great relief our little tigress once more regained her equanimity and friendly nature.

Fenella was becoming stronger and bigger every day, and the more she grew, the more boisterous she was. Stalking, which is second nature to a tiger, began to be more stealthy. This was followed by a sudden pounce in an endeavour to bring her intended 'victim' to the ground with a crafty trip. Another trick was to sneak up behind myself and other members of the family, and playfully nip our calves so that, sometimes, our legs were black and blue with bruises and before we could appear in the show, these marks had to be well hidden with suntan make-up.

At four and a half months, Fenella weighed twenty-four pounds. Her coat was becoming tawny and glossy, and her paws were large and floppy. I know it sounds strange, but Fenella had never seen another tiger. I used to think that she considered herself a child and that we, the four of us, were her parents.

People often said to me, "Won't she run away?" and I always replied. "Why should she run away? This is Fenella's home, here with us."

Although she was so much heavier, Fenella still loved to be carried, especially if the route to the circus was long, or the day was hot. She disliked walking on hot pavements and would begin to dawdle, then sit down firmly and irrevocably on the ground. This was the sign for me to pick her up and carry her. Fenella had a favourite position in my arms - this was to rest her back feet on my crooked forearm and her front paws on my shoulder. In this way she was assured of maximum comfort, and an excellent view of everything around.

In the evening, when it was cooler, Fenella would know that she was returning home, her manner alert and watchful as she padded silently by my side, straining at the leash whenever there was an intriguing shadow or unusual noise.

4

Return Voyage

When it seemed that war was inevitable between Britain and Germany everyone in the circus was upset, especially the foreign acts - which then consisted of either English or German artistes: the only Danish family had left shortly after our arrival.

Eduard Wallenda, a German, who had a sea-lion act and with whom we had all been particularly friendly, was disconsolate. He wandered restlessly about, looking more glum each day, often enquiring anxiously of us, "Are we to be friends or enemies?"

At every possible moment, with the aid of an old radio, we all strained to hear, through crackles and oscillation, the latest bulletin from England.

My heart sank as I heard that children had been evacuated from London, that Warsaw had been bombed and Danzig occupied. When war was eventually declared, pent-up emotions were released, and many women burst into tears.

After the initial shock, life in the circus resumed its normal pattern, with the exception that the German acts had to report periodically to the police as they were now in the unenviable position of being enemy aliens.

Our contract with Boswell's circus was for one year, and as the time approached when the contract would expire, we found we were faced with a difficult decision - whether to accept an offer of a further six months with the circus, or whether to return home to England. To stay on for another six months in this beautiful land of sunshine, fruit and flowers, was an alluring prospect, not to be cast away lightly but, on the other hand, our country was at war. All our relatives and loved ones were there. More and more our thoughts turned to England and our home in the Yorkshire village of Holmfirth, high up in the Pennines.

By this time the war had been in progress for six months. After the invasion of Poland by Germany on September Ist 1939, other events followed quickly. The British liner, 'Athenia', was sunk by a submarine the day after war was declared and an R.A.F. raid took place on the Kiel Canal entrance. Russian troops were mobilised, some British troops were on French soil and there had been enemy air-raids on Britain.

All this was most disturbing, both English and German members of the circus were equally distressed. Every day we discussed our problem - shall we stay, or return home? Our German friends endeavoured to persuade us to remain, telling us that we would be foolish to return to England and that the war would soon be over.

One morning my mother said with firmness and determination, "I don't know what you others are going to do, but I know what I'm going to do. I'm going home." Here was our answer, mother had decided. I breathed a sigh of relief and we all felt as though a great weight had been lifted from our shoulders. Each one of us then admitted that we had felt homesick for some time and were looking forward to going back to England.

One further problem remained – Fenella! We were all in agreement that whatever the difficulty, Fenella must return home with us. By now she was as dear to us as a child, and the thought of leaving her behind in a cage in the menagerie was quite unthinkable. We were the only parents she had known, and her affection for us equalled our love of her.

Fortunately my father came to an amicable agreement with Mr. Boswell, and after papers were signed to the effect that Mr. Boswell was no longer responsible for Fenella, she became officially ours. We were overjoyed. Whether Fenella would adapt to a new and colder climate hardly occurred to us.

Johannesburg was the last town in which we performed before leaving South Africa. The circus was booked to appear at the Rand Show - a magnificent carnival and gala - for a whole week. It was the custom, when staying for over three days in a town, for the artistes to leave the train and stay in hotels or flats. This was Fenella's first experience of living in a hotel - in fact, of living anywhere other than in a moving train - and she found it strange and exciting.

When we reached our bedroom I made a bed of rugs and blankets on the floor for Fenella, and fastened her to the bedpost at the foot of the large double bed which Meg and I were to share. Fenella was fascinated with the huge bed and spent most of the first night pouncing onto us and bouncing off again, obviously thinking that this was a new game and that we were hiding from her. We passed a hectic and sleepless night trying to quieten her, just as we were on the point of falling asleep she started pouncing again.

In the morning there was a banging at our bedroom door, opening it I found an irate man who had occupied the room below us. "What the devil was all that noise?" he stormed, "What were you doing - wrestling all night?" Apologetically, I explained that it was our tiger cub jumping about the room. His face reddened with anger and disbelief. "A likely story!" he snorted furiously. I decided it was time to invite him inside the room to see for himself.

When he saw Fenella, her eyes fixed on the door and the new arrival, his anger changed to incredulity. "Good God," he breathed, "it is a tiger!" He became so interested that his rage was forgotten and he asked if he could stroke her. "What a tale I'll have to tell them back home," he chuckled, "that a tiger kept me awake all night."

Another amusing incident occurred in the hotel. The following morning I was sitting in the bedroom writing letters when a plump, bare-footed, coloured maid entered the room quietly, carrying a tin of floor polish and a duster. She went down on her hands and knees and commenced to polish the floor, humming a native air softly to herself, her arms describing wide arcs across the wooden, parquet floor.

At first she didn't notice Fenella who, fastened to the bed, was crouching silently about three yards away from her, and she polished away happily. Suddenly she seemed to sense the cub's unblinking amber eyes fixed on her. The humming ceased and she stared at Fenella as though hypnotised. The tense staring match lasted for some seconds then the maid slowly shuffled backwards on hands and knees out of the room, leaving her polish and duster, and refusing even to come back into the hotel until "Dat animal is gone".

Meanwhile, in the backyard of the hotel, my father was busily constructing a travelling cage in readiness for the journey home. First he had taken measurements of Fenella, standing up and lying down, and then began building while allowing extra room for her to grow en route. Obviously she would have grown considerably by the time she was settled in quarantine quarters in England.

Soon the last week of the circus was over and farewells to our many dear friends were said. We had all lived in close proximity for a year and because of that, and the additional anxieties about the war, we had become very close to each other. It was with deep sorrow that we left our friends behind.

We settled ourselves into the taxi on the way to the railway station and my mother's voice became jubilant. "Do you realise," she said, "we're on our way home - we're really on our way home at last."

We travelled from Johannesburg to Cape Town in an ordinary railway train so Fenella, in her new travelling box, had to be put into the luggage van. I had asked if she could stay in our compartment but this was not permitted. Every time the train stopped I rushed to the end of the platform to the luggage van to take Fenella for a little stroll, give her food and water, or just to talk to her. She was always delighted to see me, and it was comforting to realise that although she wasn't too happy at being on her own and caged up, she was at least used to the clickety-clacking of the train and wasn't worried by its movement.

On arrival in Cape Town a car was sent by the management of the hotel to collect us. The driver seemed more than a little taken aback when I climbed in the front seat beside him and pulled Fenella on to my lap. He sat rigid and tense, driving as quickly as he dared through the town without uttering a word or giving a sideways glance at the tiger. As we all dismounted he slowly breathed a sigh of relief. He had carried unusual passengers before, but never - ever - a live tiger.

We all knew of the wondrous beauty of Cape Town and had hoped to have a few days' holiday there before leaving South Africa. I particularly wished to explore and climb up Table Mountain, whose rocky splendour we had often seen in the distance. Much to our disappointment we learned that the ship was due to sail in two days. There was much to attend to - especially in relation to Fenella - and we were anxious in case all the formalities would not be completed when the ship sailed. We spent frustrating hours in Cooks offices attending to last minute details.

It was essential to obtain a certificate of health for Fenella. It was arranged for a vet to call at the hotel to inspect her. This was the first time the vet had ever had to deal with young tigers, and he made it very clear that he did not trust our young tigress. He regarded Fenella suspiciously for a while, standing at a safe distance from her. Fenella, quite unaware of his scrutiny, was playing happily around a garden seat on the 'stoep' (built-up verandah) of the hotel. Finally the vet spoke, in a ponderous manner, "She looks a very healthy animal," he remarked, "if she should have any trouble with hair-ball in the stomach, give her a whole pigeon with its feathers on." I could hardly suppress my laughter at the thought of Fenella's reaction if she was presented with a dead pigeon to eat, with or without feathers! The vet then wrote out the precious bill of health, collected his fee of one guinea and departed on his way.

Friday 29th March, 1940, was our last day in South Africa. We made way to the docks to board the 'Arundel Castle', and found her looking unpainted and dirty as part of her war-time camouflage. I thought sadly how different she looked from her spruce sister, the 'Windsor Castle', in which we had travelled to South Africa.

Up to that moment I had assumed that Fenella would be taken on board in the usual manner of all baggage, that is, that she, in her box, would be hoisted on board by a crane. However, as I stood on the quay, Fenella beside me on her lead, and watched the baggage being loaded, swinging dizzily aloft against the blue of the sky, the crane screeching, I felt that this was no way for our tiger cub to go on board. Besides, Fenella would be terrified at suddenly finding herself whisked high up in space. The gangway was close at hand, it was a safe one with canvas sides. "Come along, Fenny," I said and, watched by the curious expressions of the passengers who were peering at us over the ship's rail, I calmly led the tiger past the officer examining the tickets, who seemed too amused, or surprised, to protest.

Twin anti-aircraft guns had been mounted on the after deck of the 'Arundel Castle', and next to these was Fenella's travelling box. It didn't seem to be a really suitable place for Fenella, I thought, as I covered her box with a protective sheet of tarpaulin; still, it was better than having her kept below in the hold.

A slight sea mist swirled damply around the ship and this, combined with the complete blackout on board - our first experience of this - resulted in an eerie feeling as we surged and throbbed into the night. It seemed as if we were truly voyaging into the unknown.

I stood, gazing over the rail, watching the phosphorescent gleam of our wake, happy to be returning home even though the country was at war, but sad to be leaving South Africa, where I had spent such a happy year.

At breakfast the following day, my father was surprised to receive a personal note from the captain. How pleased we all were to learn that Fenella's box was to be transferred to the second class sun deck and that this small upper deck was to be for her exclusive use. The box was placed between two large packing cases, which were rumoured to contain aeroplane parts. Deck hands soon rigged up a canvas awning to keep off the heat of the tropical sun and fixed a 'private' notice at the top of the companion stairway. The tiger cub was really getting V. I. P. treatment, but this may have been due to the small number of passengers on board the ship. The threat of war, in which we were all involved, may also have been responsible for the free and easy atmosphere on the ship.

The ship was not in convoy, but sped through the ocean on a zig-zag course. It was hoped that in this way she would be too fast for German U-boats to catch unless, by cruel fate, our paths chanced to coincide. In case this happened, the life-boats were carried permanently slung overboard on their davits.

From time to time the ack-ack crew had gun practice, firing off several rounds into the blue beyond. The captain, showing a fine concern for Fenella, used to send notes to my father informing him when these practice shoots were scheduled, so that we would be close in case the cub was frightened by the noise. At first I was somewhat worried but my fears proved groundless. Fenella took no more notice of the gunshots than she had of the shunting and bumping of the trains in which she had spent her first six months.

We soon established a regular routine. On those sparkling bright mornings, on decks still wet from their earlier sluicing, and before the other passengers were about on their pre-breakfast promenade, we would be on the sun deck with

Fenella. I held a large wad of newspaper as kitty litter trying to get her house trained as I took her for her morning constitutional walk round and round the deck.

The presence of a tiger cub created an interesting diversion for all on board the ship, and during the day almost everyone used to climb the companion stairway to enquire about her. They usually stayed to watch Fenella's antics as she played, rolled or frolicked on the deck, she was almost perpetually chasing one or other of us.

Fenella with Meg & Dad sitting in the sun

Like all young animals she had this curious mixture of intense activity before she flopped down with exhaustion, only waiting to rally her strength before resuming her chasing. At this time she was like a mixture of a kitten and a very boisterous puppy. She was about the height of a Labrador dog, although her paws and shoulders were bigger than those of any dog. She would wrestle, bite without being vicious, and use her claws without seeking to hurt. She was still small enough to be controlled, except when she was feeling particularly playful, when controlling and fending her off became a full time occupation. To Fenella, this was all part of a glorious game, and only made her more excited and eager to attack. As lion and tiger cubs often wrestle with each other and take part in mock fights, Fenella was only behaving naturally.

Fenella's favourite visitor was the ship's butcher. He used to arrive at mid-day with dishes of delicious cooked meats, bones and milky puddings. Then he stood watching her eat, his homely face wreathed in a smile of satisfaction. No chef de cuisine could have found more pleasure from watching the most fastidious gourmet eating a personally prepared meal. But the greatest moment for the butcher was after Fenella had eaten as much as she wanted, for then she gave her undivided attention to him. I must confess that it was not the man himself who fascinated Fenella, it was rather his long blue and white striped apron which was the attraction. To tease Fenella the butcher used to flip his apron up and down and the cub, like an oversized kitten, tried to catch it in her paws. There was great excitement and when Fenella succeeded she then gripped the apron firmly in her teeth and a tug of war ensued. Sometimes the butcher used to pretend not to notice that Fenella was there, then the tiger cub warily circled him, sneaked up behind him, and gave her butcher friend a sharp nip on the rear. Instead of alarming the man, this really made his day. The young tiger had early realised that the most effective way to attack was to spring from behind.

Many of Fenella's antics amused us immensely, but the funniest of all was the cub's persistent attempts to sit in a deck chair. It seemed to puzzle her that we could all sit in one with so much comfort, when it was so difficult for the young tigress to accommodate herself in that awkward, sagging, canvas chair. Her tail was too long and got in her way. She tried manoeuvering herself carefully round, lying first on one side, then on the other, draping her limp paws over the edge of the chair and washing them vigorously. Eventually she decided there must be a more comfortable and cooler place for a young tiger's siesta, and awkwardly clambered off the precarious deck chair to flop down in the shade of the ship's locker.

Soon we had left Las Palmas behind, still ablaze with light, as the ship continued in the dark ocean in complete black out, the only light being from the canopy of bright, twinkling stars. Once again we could see the constellation of the Great Bear swinging round the North Star. We were nearing England, we were nearly home.

I began to wonder what friends and neighbours would think when we arrived home with a tiger cub. What would our relatives think, some of whom had spent their quiet and seemingly uneventful lives in a small Yorkshire village; some of them had never been further than Blackpool or Scarborough. They already considered us a "bit odd" being "on the stage".

One cousin had written to us in South Africa and had added a postscript, "Bring back a monkey". Obviously, he would be greatly amused. But another friend, whom we had told about our mutual pet, had sent us a cartoon depicting Hitler first as a tiger cub, then growing into an enormous ferocious tiger. It didn't seem a very good omen and was an undoubted warning of what he expected.

Almost fearfully I knelt beside the travelling crate and felt inside, gently stroking the soft, warm fur of the tiger cub. Immediately I felt her respond to my caress as she stretched with languor to the very tips of her claws, then sighed contentedly, relaxed, and fell asleep again. It didn't seem possible that such a delightful, affectionate creature could ever become wild and ferocious. I sighed deeply - we could only wait and see.

Fenella with Dad, almost home, wrapped in travelling rug, weather is chilly

Meanwhile there was always plenty of activity on board. Ocean liners are geared to keeping the passengers happy and no war was going to deter them. In spite of the strict blackout above deck, parties, games and dances continued below. Love affairs, quarrels and reconciliations took place. Many of the passengers were given nicknames; one lady - because of her flamboyant dress and long golden earrings - was quite naturally referred to as 'the gypsy'. It came as a surprise, however, on the last day of the voyage, to discover that my sister and I were known throughout the ship as 'Tiger Lily' and 'Panther Peg'.

As the ship surged up the Channel into the haven of Southampton water, I breathed a sigh of thankfulness. We had arrived safely and without trouble.

5

Fenella - In Quarantine

But trouble lurked ahead in the shape of officialdom, and the problem of quarantine for Fenella.

As the ship docked at Southampton, we were met by a representative of the Travel Agency who informed us solemnly that there had been a hitch, and that the necessary permit to land Fenella was not available. Until the permit arrived she was to be confined to the ship. "You must remember," the agent said gravely, "there's a war on." For a time there seemed the awful possibility, conditions being as they were, that Fenella might spend the formative years of her life travelling to and from South Africa on the 'Arundel Castle'. If, by chance, the ship was requisitioned for troops - well, anything might happen.

An urgent family conference was held whilst we anxiously discussed what we should do about this unexpected dilemma. Our main problem was going to be the period of quarantine, the next six months. Ideally, it was important for Fenella to remain as close to us as practicable so that we could spend the maximum amount of time with her. This period of confinement could well prove a most crucial time. Fenella had been with us from birth and unless we were there to feed her, play with her, and give her the love and companionship she expected during this quarantine period, we feared we might lose the happy relationship that we had built up.

My mother and I decided to continue the journey to Yorkshire and see if we could find suitable accommodation there for our tiger cub, whilst my father and Meg remained on the ship in Southampton.

Two days later, the landing permit arrived and at last we were allowed to take Fenella off the ship. With the permit came instructions that the tiger should be initially quarantined in authorised kennels at Watford until a more suitable place was approved. My father returned home to assist us in the fruitless search for a convenient place in which to quarantine a young tiger, while Meg and Fenella travelled to Watford.

Now Meg, who had found lodgings near the kennels, became full time nursemaid to an energetic young tiger cub - or should it be kennel-maid?

The owners of the kennels were faced with a problem; they had never had a tiger before. The kennel man was afraid that the scent of a tiger might upset his dogs and suggested that Fenella's box should be put into a nearby garage. This, with a grassy run adjoining it, became her home for the next four weeks.

Out in the run, during the cool spring days of early April, with fresh green grass beneath her feet, Fenella became an increasingly boisterous young tiger. She was getting bigger and stronger, and her energy seemed to be boundless. For one person, she was more than a handful and was often difficult to manage.

It wasn't that she had become wicked or bad-tempered, but the young tiger was going through an aggressive period and had become exceedingly playful. It was her strength and energy which now presented a problem. When the family were together we could take turns in playing with her, but when all her attentions were perpetually channelled in one direction, that poor person had a difficult time from a young tiger continually demanding attention. Fenella remained loving and affectionate as well as playful, but she did not realise her own strength and sought to utilise her vast resources of energy in tiger games.

The flit spray was still a potent weapon, no longer filled with noxious insect or nit repellent fluid but simply clean water. Usually, even the fine spray of water was not required; the sight and sound of the spray was enough to send her slinking away. It was not, however, always successful. There were occasions when, in desperation, Meg had to grab Fenella's throat and hold her down until she finally gave up her efforts to attack and maul my poor sister. But Fenella didn't resent this treatment. To her it was part of the game of life and growing up. I can only suppose that in her native habitat, if she had annoyed her own mother, the adult female tiger would also have used her superior strength to subdue her unruly cub.

Fenella was also losing her baby teeth and her adult teeth were pushing through her gums. As a result, she chewed anything within range and wasn't particularly worried what she chewed. Large holes were gnawed in her travelling rugs and blankets as she ate, with evident relish, the tough, woolly, material. The curious addition to her diet didn't seem to harm her and may well have done her digestion some good. In all probability, wild tigers would eat fur and skin as they gorge on their kill.

Meg was not amused when she discovered that Fenella - who, for a time had been behaving quietly, giving Meg a well-earned rest - had, in fact, been contentedly gnawing a large hole in the back of her tweed coat.

Feeding Fenella became another problem from the moment we set foot in England. In South Africa and on board the ship meat had been plentiful, but in Britain it was the commencement of rationing and tigers didn't have ration books. However, Meg managed quite well with her landlady's butcher as rationing was at that time not as rigid as later on in the war. The butcher's allocation then was more adequate to meet his customer's requirements and certain meats, such as oxtails, could be bought without ration coupons.

The kennel man, who was supposed to provide Fenella's food, tried to be helpful but the young tigress was more fastidious concerning her diet than his other charges. When he brought her a cooked beast's heart, Fenella refused disdainfully even to look at it. She was used to tasty stews and cooked mince, and the diet of the kennels wasn't recognisable as food.

Fortunately Meg had provided herself with a paraffin Valor stove, anticipating that she might have to cook Fenella's meals. Each day she bought minced beef, stewing steak - in fact, anything she could obtain from the shop - which she augmented with vegetables or spaghetti into appetising stews which the two of them shared. Fenella, despite being a young tiger cub, never objected to receiving 'the lion's share'.

Besides often being a hungry tiger, Fenella continued to be a destructive one. A note in Meg's diary records: "My brown woollen skirt must be rotten. Fenny has torn it three times and bitten a piece right out of it."

On one occasion, one of Meg's boyfriends travelled to Watford to see her, and as they discussed life and talked of the things young lovers discuss, Fenella quietly chewed a hole in his car rug. It is hardly surprising that the romance never blossomed.

During those four weeks, Meg spent practically the whole of each day, from breakfast until six or seven o'clock - sometimes as late as nine p.m. - at the kennels, just keeping a young, over-active tiger company. She was battered and bruised by Fenella's rough play and had more than one scar where the claws of her boisterous pet had penetrated her slacks and scarred her thighs.

At home in Yorkshire, the fruitless search for a suitable quarantine place continued. Each day we became more downcast but my father, ever resourceful, suddenly thought of a wonderful idea. As we couldn't find suitable quarantine quarters, why should we not create our own? If local council approval could be obtained, why not convert our own back garden into suitable quarantine quarters?

Fired with enthusiasm, my father applied to the local council who, with no seeming reluctance, granted the application. Plans were hastily drawn. A large hut was obtained as sleeping and living quarters. Plants and shrubs in the garden were uprooted, a herbaceous border was ruthlessly destroyed, and daily the garden resounded with frantic hammering and sawing as a cage front was fitted and an aperture made in the hut side. Inside the hut itself, my father erected an entrance cage, into which you stepped from the outside door. When the door was closed behind you it was then possible to open the door from the entrance cage into the hut itself; this was the tiger's lair. The main advantage was that you could let yourself into the hut whilst preventing a lively, striped bundle of mischief escaping into the open air and the freedom Fenella would doubtless desire.

On the lawn in front of the hut, and attached to it, there was a compound twenty-one feet long by fifteen feet wide, the length of the hut, and six feet high. This had to comply with the specific requirements demanded by the laws of quarantine. It had to be surrounded and covered over with a double thickness of strong mesh chain link netting, with an interweaving space of three inches between the two nettings, thus ensuring that no animal on the outside could come in contact with the caged animal. Even to touch noses in a friendly sniff was forbidden.

The hut was installed and the compound completed within a month. Leading from the hut to the compound was the aperture which could be caged off with a barred door and also sealed off with a sliding door to keep out the cold of the night air. Relieved that at last the hard, strenuous work had been completed, we surveyed the results and felt justifiably proud of what we had achieved, but the next step was the crucial one. We stood around with baited breath when the Man from the Ministry arrived or, to give him his full title, the Inspector from the Ministry of Agriculture and Fisheries. This was an unusual experience for the inspector, who had rarely been asked to inspect quarantine accommodation in someone's back garden, and still less for a tiger from South Africa.

The inspector seemed quite impressed with the hut. He approved of the double bars, the double doors, and the double netting on the compound. He looked troubled though and obviously had some misgivings. We looked at each other anxiously, had we done something wrong? Thoughtfully, and speaking slowly, the inspector wondered if the tiger could burrow her way under the netting.

We assured him earnestly that Fenella had never shown any desire to burrow holes, that tigers were not great burrowers, and that, in any case, our netting, in duplicate, was buried deep in the ground. Slowly, he signed the important document - the form approving the quarantine arrangements. He would have been a hard man to convince if we'd been importing moles.

As for Meg in Watford, battered and bruised and worn out with long days with Fenella, she was certainly pleased when the news came that the building and compound had passed Ministry inspection, and that Fenella could at last be brought home. As quickly as possible, Meg arranged for the L.M. S. to collect and deliver them to Euston Station, London.

At the station, Fenella's box was placed on a trolley and trundled along the platform. They had arrived early and the train was not yet in the station. Fenella had settled down in her box and was resting, so Meg quietly tucked the tarpaulin around the box and hurried along to the buffet for a welcome cup of tea.

On returning she found, to her dismay, that two curious soldiers had untied the tarpaulin and were teasing the tiger cub by poking her with a stick. Poor Fenella, her eyes were wild and black with rage as she spat and snarled at them to avoid the prodding stick.

Furiously, Meg dashed up to them, screaming angrily, "What on earth do you think you're doing, you cruel monsters?" She snatched the stick from them and almost hit them with it. Sheepishly, the soldiers shuffled away, muttering something about...only finding out if it was a real one!

After that traumatic experience, Meg decided to travel in the guard's van to prevent thoughtless and curious persons from further disturbing the cub who, by then, was distraught at the unexpected attack. For some time afterwards she lifted the corners of her mouth and spat at nothing in particular.

The luggage van contained a mixed consignment, including two greyhounds and a large pram with six month old twins. The mother of the twins had found a seat farther up the train and, apparently unconcerned, had left them to share the luggage van with the greyhounds and a tiger cub. To be fair, she did return from time to time to ensure that her offspring were still alive and well.

The train rattled and clattered on its journey northwards. The greyhounds, not at all happy, howled dismally; the babies whimpered and cried, whereas the tiger cub - back in an element in which she had grown up - was happy to hear the familiar clanking and swaying of the train. Poor Meg, her tasks seemed endless. Her own charge, having recovered from one ordeal, Meg found herself playing nursemaid to the two greyhounds and twin babies. It was possible that the presence of a young tiger failed to reassure the greyhounds. I discovered later that dogs meeting Fenella for the first time became perturbed and even panic-stricken.

I had not seen Fenella for four weeks and a strange feeling of excitement and tenseness came over me as I waited on Huddersfield platform with my mother and father. Naturally, I imagined Fenella to be as l had last seen her in Southampton. I expected her face still to have its short flat fur around the jaws, squared off like an Airedale dog. But when she was carried out of the train and onto the platform, I was struck immediately by the considerable change in her appearance.

Fenella had grown, and her box now appeared too small. But the most surprising change, to me, was the ruff of fur which had grown around her face, making her look less like an overgrown kitten and more like a real tiger.

For a moment my heart quailed. I felt almost afraid of this bigger, brighter young tiger, with beautiful black and tawny striped flanks and glowing amber eyes. Softly I spoke her name, "Fenny, Fenny." Almost immediately she responded with a short chuckling sound which is a tiger's voice of friendship and affection. I knew then that all was well and that our Fenny was still the same friendly cub we had so patiently reared and grown to love.

It was difficult carrying her box into the garden as she was getting heavier all the time. How much easier it would have been if she had been allowed to walk. Fenella was becoming quite excited, and rubbed her face against the netting of the box, trying to make contact with our fingers, as we struggled to carry the box to its final destination. It was obvious that the tiger remembered each one of us and was delighted to see us all again.

As soon as the door was safely fastened and the box in position, I opened the door of her travelling box and she leaped eagerly into the hut that was to be her home for the next five months. It was just like old times. Fenella rubbed against each of us in turn, whilst she chuckled and moaned softly with ecstatic pleasure at being with her family again. Next she walked round each in turn, again and again, giving this, and other evidence of her affection.

It was late and almost dark before Fenella settled down to sleep, and it was typical of her that she had a firm hold on the sleeve of my father's jacket as he lay on the hut floor with his head and shoulders inside her travelling box - for she had selected this familiar venue as her sleeping place. She was determined not to be left alone again. She had objected to Meg leaving her at night-time in Watford and now that she was back with her family she was going to ensure that this would not recur. In the end, sleep overcame the tired animal. My father carefully disengaged his sleeve from Fenny's grasp and slowly, silently, stole towards the door of the hut to let himself into the intervening locking chamber. To his surprise he found that his sleeping tiger had even more silently passed him in the gloom and was there, waiting for him to open the door.

6

Quarantine Continued

A number of wild animals are very fussy about their toilet habits, showing a decided preference for some particular spot, and Fenella was quick to choose a corner within the hut out of sight of onlookers. It was amusing to see her disappear in a most modest manner, when attending to the call of nature.

For easier cleaning purposes, we lined the floor in this corner with a covering of zinc, then quickly shovelled up her droppings which were buried in the garden.

For the first few weeks this method was quite satisfactory, but our garden (or should I say - what was left of it, now that it contained a hut and a compound) wasn't very large, and soon there were no areas of ground left. There were little mounds of earth everywhere, and it began to look as though, besides a young tigress, we had a crazy mole in residence.

It was evident a better method had to be found, and quickly too. Half-jokingly, the suggestion was made that Fenella be potty-trained; surprisingly, this seemingly ludicrous idea was successful. Fenella was used to newspapers being placed underneath her, and a container was only one step further; to our relief, she made no objection. This was, in fact, one of the main reasons why Fenella was able to live in the house as a member of the family on termination of the period of quarantine.

Kassie & Meg with Fenella in the back garden

Although Fenella had thrived exceedingly well on a diet of cooked meats and stews, it was not the correct diet for a tiger. As a carnivore she should be eating raw meat, and at this stage it seemed important to transfer her to her inherently natural diet.

Meat was becoming more and more difficult to obtain, but shops selling horsemeat for human consumption were opening in nearby towns. This meat was free of coupons, so it was decided to try Fenny on horsemeat.

I wondered what her reaction would be to this change of diet, as I remembered with some alarm the behaviour of the wild animals and menagerie beasts in the circus, who had snarled and growled with ferocity when they received their portion of raw meat. Could this possibly produce the same ferocity in our affectionate cub?

For her next meal, I put some raw meat in the dish in which she normally ate her stews. By doing that I hoped she might associate the dish's contents with her usual food. Fenella was obviously interested in the dish but quite nonplussed by its contents. She sniffed at the meat curiously, wondering what it could be. Then she walked nonchalantly away from the dish and continued her perambulations - which any caged animal does to obtain the exercise its instinct tells it is necessary - backwards and forwards to the end of the hut.

"Good girl," said my father encouragingly, tapping the dish as he spoke and picking it up and putting it down again. The noise was sufficient to attract Fenella to the dish again, and once more she sniffed at it curiously. Evidently it was a strange odour to her delicate nostrils, for she put her head up, wrinkled her nose and curled her lips in what looked like a horse laugh. Then, to show her displeasure, she stuck her tongue out in a rude gesture and resumed her pacing up and down the hut, wondering what had happened to her usual lunch.

Not defeated, my father tried again. Once more he rattled the dish and put it down, and once more his tactics attracted Fenella to the dish. She sniffed at it a third time, then with a look of complete disgust, hit the dish with her paw and sent the meat slithering all across the wooden floor.

Clearly Fenella did not associate raw meat with food, but my father was a resourceful man. He took the large chunk of raw meat and with a sharp knife cut off a small piece. The next time Fenny padded towards him, he threw an arresting arm over her back, and whilst he held her, pushed the morsel of raw meat into her mouth, between her black lips at the rear of her mouth behind her fangs, and tried to get it to the molars. Fenella appeared surprised, and even indignant, at this unexpected attempt to force-feed her. She backed away quickly, opened her mouth and the piece of meat fell on the floor. A further attempt was equally unsuccessful as Fenella again forced the meat out with her tongue. Fenella clearly didn't like this treatment and was beginning to look hurt and very sorry for herself. It seemed that we had a problem tiger on our hands. How were we going to get her to eat raw meat when she didn't recognise it as food?

"We could try disguising it," suggested Meg, "after all, if you were offered raw meat after eating nothing but warm cooked food, you wouldn't know what it was, would you?" There seemed a lot of sense in this remark and Meg continued. "Young tigers see their parents eat raw meat and learn from them. Fenny has never seen us eat raw meat, and I'm not starting to eat it now just to teach her." Meg's logic was brilliant, and we all wondered why we had not thought of this. Of course raw meat must seem cold comfort after hot dinners.

Quickly, I returned to the house with the mutilated meat, which I chopped into small pieces and put in the frying pan. Then I seared the meat gently in a little butter, poured melted butter over it and hurried back to the hut.

Fenella was still pacing hungrily up and down, but as soon as she smelled the tantalizing odour of melted butter wafting her way she showed immediate interest. I put the dish of meat in front of her and stood back expecting her to gobble the appetising morsels in front of her. To my surprise she began to lick the butter delicately, and leave the meat!

Again my father tried to force-feed pieces of meat into the side of her mouth and at last, perhaps because the butter made it more palatable, she slowly began to chew it. Providing the meat was impregnated with butter, which she adored, Fenella began to accept it but showed no sign of eagerness, as she did for the cooked food to which she was accustomed. For a long time she refused to eat the meat without some form of camouflage. Later, she began to enjoy it although it had to be fresh meat, and preferably warm.

Bones, however, were a totally different matter. Fenella loved gnawing bones; so it may well be that the old adage 'the nearer the bone the sweeter the meat' really does apply. Certainly the young tigress seemed to think so, and she was really delighted by the large thighbones we obtained for her. Fenny was very possessive about bones, and often growled at them like a really wild animal, licking and pawing them as she walked around snarling softly.

It is a strange fact that semi-tame animals in circus cages, and who often accept human handling, will never allow meat to be taken from them. They will snarl and defend their meat fiercely and almost certainly attack anyone, even their familiar and friendly trainers, if they try to rob them of their meat.

Fenella, however, never objected to us taking away her meat. I think she had sufficient faith that we should restore it in adequate quantity to assuage her hunger. Occasionally, when she was out of quarantine and my father was cutting up her meat in the house, she would sneak up and make off with a thirty pound piece from which my father was cutting her daily ration. Fenella always allowed it to be taken from her without demur, but did not have the same attitude to bones. She reluctantly permitted us to take them from her if we firmly insisted. It seemed that a bone represented some part of a 'kill' to her instincts, whereas lumps of raw meat had a different association.

We were not able to give her many bones as they were bulky and difficult to bring back from Huddersfield on a crowded bus (petrol being rationed) with a heavy load of raw horse-meat. Usually a bone was given to her after she had eaten her meat, then she would crouch over it, grasping it firmly under her front paws and initially licking off all the fragments of meat with her rough, rasping tongue. Then she chewed the gristle with her powerful back molars, using first one side of the mouth, then the other. If one approached too close, Fenella flattened her ears and growled menacingly - a deep growl, originating far down her throat and an unmistakable warning to keep away. Usually it was deemed more prudent to leave the cub undisturbed with her bone. If for some reason or other we decided to take it from her, she would protest and hang on to it by tooth and claw, but despite all her threats and growls she never attacked us.

Our back garden sloped upwards away from the house, and Fenella's hut had been erected at the top of the slope, with the run extending in front of it and down the garden towards the house. This vantage point provided Fenella with a good view of the house. As she was on the same level as the back downstairs window, the tiger could watch us whenever interested. In fact, Fenella was extremely interested and kept the house under almost perpetual surveillance, watching the family's comings and goings with great excitement.

It wasn't long before the news leaked out that there was a young tigress in our back garden, and soon there was a stream of visitors. Most of them knocked at the door and asked if they could see the tiger, but as we lived in a terraced house - each pair being separated by a covered passage leading to the back - it was possible to creep up the 'tunnel' unobserved and without asking.

Four o'clock was usually the peak viewing hour as the local school is only about two hundred yards further up the hill from our house. Our back garden became a favourite calling place for the children as soon as they left school.

First there would be a scuffling and scraping of shoes along the passage, followed by excited whispers: "You go ask," we would hear a small voice say. "No, you go," hissed another one. Eventually one of the more adventurous, or a child who had already been, used to creep forward until they caught a glimpse of the wired off compound in the garden. If the answer was "Yes, I can see it," there was a wild surge forward of young bodies, all eager to see the tiger. This was followed by a knock on the back door and a request to see Fenella, whilst excited voices in West Riding dialect called out: "Sithee - it's theer. Look where I told thee!" and the rush up the garden began, from scores of little boys and girls, all of them agog to see the young tigress. Fenella was equally pleased to see the children. She loved company and wanted more than anything to come out of the enclosure and play with her new friends.

To alleviate the boredom her restricted world produced, we were continually trying to devise ways of amusing her. She loved anything that made a noise or clattered as she carried or dragged it around. I gave her a galvanised bucket and an enamel bowl which rattled when she sent it flying along the floor of her pen. A never failing source of interest was a tin can containing a few stones, the lid of which was securely fastened. This, Fenella pawed and propelled around the pen; she pushed it, leaped on it, held it firmly in her paws, pushed it away again, and then pounced on it once more, excited by its continual rattle.

She was also extremely fond of a large, variegated broom bush which had been uprooted when the garden was cleared for her pen. This had been put inside her compound and Fenny obtained great pleasure from dragging it all over her territory. She rattled it against the compound wire then pretended to hide behind it before leaping out to pounce on whichever one of us was in the compound with her.

One day Meg and I decided to teach Fenny a few tricks but we had no idea how to set about it. I had watched wild animal trainers in splendid uniforms, crack whips and use chairs to fend off ferocious looking lions before getting them to climb on to pedestals and form themselves into pyramids, or to leap from one pedestal to another. Sometimes the trainer would make them all lie down side by side. I had also seen Togare, the famous lion tamer, stand with a lion round his shoulders and then put his head in the lion's mouth. These tricks were excellent but how did they get the animals to agree to take their parts in the routine?

Cracking whips at Fenella didn't seem the right approach. She was far too friendly and would only wonder what on earth we were doing. We wanted Fenella to remain friendly but nevertheless there seemed no reason why she shouldn't be persuaded to perform little tricks.

So Meg and I made some pedestals from orange boxes - we found this far from easy. Then we rigged up a kind of tightrope by suspending a beam four inches wide between two tables. When these were fixed up, we commenced the training course. Fenella, who was always interested in anything we did, found this activity fascinating and, as usual, succeeded in getting in the way. However, she was at a complete loss to understand what part, if any, she was to play in the proceeding.

We endeavoured to make it clear just what was expected of our tiger pet by enticing her with her favourite tit-bit, taken from our precious butter ration, melted in a saucer and placed temptingly in front of her nose. The smell of the butter was irresistible to Fenella and, as I slowly drew the saucer away from her nose she moved after it; great excitement - as she jumped over the pedestals, neck outstretched and tongue curling in anticipation of the melted butter. Fenella, as though mesmerised, followed the butter like a donkey following a dangling carrot, and surprised us by walking right along the beam, something she did with consummate ease.

Meg and I were getting more and more enthusiastic. Flushed with success, we persuaded Fenny to repeat the performance and walk across the precarious beam a second time. Perhaps it was going to be easier than we had thought to train a young tigress! When Fenella completed the 'act' for a third time, we were convinced we were witnessing the early development of a new star.

Suddenly, the bubble burst, and our dreams of being famous animal trainers were shattered. Fenella, who sometimes showed a contrary streak, decided not to cooperate any longer at this 'silly game'. I think it must have occurred to her that she was being conned into doing something that she didn't want to do, and at the end of her effort, the melted butter was no nearer. With a show of petulance more befitting to a small spoilt child than a lordly animal, she threw herself on the floor and thrashed her tail backwards and forwards disapprovingly. No amount of further bribery would induce Fenny to try again. Training tigers wasn't so easy after all we decided disappointedly.

Fenella, in the meantime, continued to grow bigger and bigger as the period of quarantine was nearly ended.

It was about this time that my favourite aunt came to visit us. I was longing to show her my wonderful pet, and as soon as greetings were concluded I took her into our garden.

Fenny was pacing up and down her wired-off compound and, delighted to see us, she padded forward, rubbing her face against the netting.

My aunt gazed at Fenella with awe and I felt she was impressed by her. I was happy to think she appreciated, as I did, the rich gold colour of the tiger's striped flanks, the lustre of her coat and the lithe grace of her measured gait.

"Well?" I asked expectantly, eager to hear her expressions of admiration; but as I looked into her face, I could see that her look had become one of horror. My heart sank within me as I realised that my aunt had no liking for our lovely young tigress. Almost bitterly she said, "Well, Kassie, you've brought this creature home with you. All I can say..." she muttered almost under her breath, "I hope it won't live long!"

7

Freedom

I won't easily forget the day that Fenny's quarantine period came to an end. October 15th, 1940, was a fine and breezy morning which started the same as any other day, except that there was a feeling of anticipation, of suppressed excitement, in the air. Perhaps it was my imagination, but even Fenella seemed to sense that something was different as she padded around the run. For six months Fenella had been a caged animal in the garden, and now we were eager to take her into the house without any further delay.

I stroked her lovingly as l fastened the new leather, brass-studded collar around her neck and attached it to a stout steel chain lead. Although I felt reasonably confident that she would take this new move to freedom in her stride, it was essential to take all precautions. My heart began to beat quickly as I opened the hut door and led her, rather hesitantly at first, down the garden path; but Fenella had no doubt at all in which direction she was heading; she had stared longingly at the house door for so long that this had become her ultimate aim, now she hurried forward, pulling strongly on the lead.

Fenella was now a year old, and usually a lion or tiger cub kept as a pet would, by this time, be consigned to a zoo. It was not without some trepidation that we waited to observe her reactions as she entered the house for the first time.

But Fenella's behaviour was quite composed, she accepted this change in her life unquestioningly as she had accepted so many previous changes. Not surprisingly, she was intrigued and curious, and immediately carried out a thorough examination of all the furniture in the room, sniffing at chairs, placing her paws on the table to get an all-over view, and in no time at all she had made herself completely at home by settling comfortably on the couch, which she decided, then and there, was to be her future throne.

From this time onwards, Fenella spent a great deal of time in the house. She was growing up quickly and had become a much more dignified young lady. As tigers are not fully grown until they are two and a half years old, it is difficult to compare her size then with a dog. A tiger is so much longer in the body and has larger paws, but as for her height, I should say she was then as tall as a St. Bernard. I felt thankful she was a Sumatran tiger, as they are one of the smallest breeds, although they are reputed to be the most ferocious.

Fenella on her favourite couch

Inquisitive creature that she was, Fenella adored being in the house; there was so much more to see and do. She discovered a new and exciting delight in going upstairs to inspect the bedrooms and the beds, all of which she found much to her liking.

She discovered pillows - large plump ones, stuffed with feathers. Using one of her paws with utmost delicacy, she used to scoop the bedclothes down as neatly as a person using his or her hands, pick up a pillow in her mouth, and then bring it downstairs. But even tigers have their problems: as our staircase is very steep, and as a tiger drags its prey under its body, the acute angle at which Fenella came downstairs, forced her to sit on the pillow. Her pads, shiny and slippery as polished leather, lost control and Fenny, reluctant to let go of the pillow, slid and bumped like a toboggan and landed in a tumbled heap at the bottom of the stairs. Not at all deterred, she then walked proudly around the room carrying her trophy as high as possible in order not to trip over it. The beloved pillow was then enveloped in her paws, and Fenella crouched over it, gnawing open the pillow corners. It was obvious that she thought this was a great game as she scattered the feathers everywhere, but Meg and I thought otherwise after collecting, with difficulty, hundreds of feathers and re-sewing several pillow corners. We decided we must be firm and that Fenella must be banned, as far as possible, from going upstairs. To make the ban effective, we tried to keep the bedroom doors closed, but of course sometimes we forgot.

This led to a mad race up the stairs to close the bedroom doors before Fenella could get there; this proved practically impossible as, when pursued, Fenella could mount the stairs in three large bounds. Fortunately, she invariably wandered into the bathroom first and peered interestedly down the loo, thus providing us with the opportunity to close the other doors - then, to amaze her, I flushed the loo.

Although Fenny was getting bigger and heavier all the time, she still loved to pounce on Meg and I when we were in bed. My father, who had an impish sense of humour, knew that Meg and I were reluctant to get up early during the weekend, so he used to fetch Fenella from her hut and bring her to the foot of the stairs. Through my hazy sleep, I would hear him say, "Go on, lassie, go and get them up." In a moment, Fenella's inquisitive head appeared round the bedroom door (open again) and as we agitated the blankets, there was a quick movement as the tiger pounced on us with a mighty bound; we had to brace our bodies stiffly against the impact of the heavy body. This was a great game, and Fenella loved it; eventually, to make our escape, we threw all the covers over her.

Another favourite place was the cellar. Whenever the opportunity presented itself, Fenella would be off down the stone steps into the dark room to gaze with delight at the huge joints of horsemeat hanging on hooks from the low ceiling.

Although Fenella still loved to play, her behaviour was slowly becoming more restrained. She spent much time in sitting majestically on the couch and washing herself. Fenella was inordinately proud of her appearance and took hours cleaning and grooming herself, particularly after feeding. First she washed her face and whiskers with a paw, then her gleaming flanks with long, sweeping strokes of her rough tongue; her paws too had to be dealt with and were licked vigorously on top, between the toes and under the pads, any pieces of rough skin on the pads were nibbled away. If any of the family happened to sit next to her during these ablutions, she always obliged by giving them a few sand-papery licks as a friendly gesture.

Fenella, always curious, watched attentively all the movements in the house. When anyone knocked at the door she was nearly always there first. To those callers who were unaware of the tiger's presence this was a great shock, when the door was opened not only by my mother but by an inquisitive tiger. Salesmen completely forgot their sales talk, and almost their goods, as they hurried away. How were they to know that Fenella, unlike some dogs, was always warmly disposed towards them? One persistent salesman, who had managed to put his foot in the doorway and was talking unceasingly, suddenly became conscious of something pushing against his leg. His eyes looked as if they would pop out of his head as he stared in disbelief at the large, striped creature looking up at him. However, he wasted no time and, muttering to himself, he grabbed his case and ran!

Fenella could never resist playing 'Cat and Mouse' with Meg and myself, perhaps it was because we invariably ran quickly up and down the stairs. The sound of our swift footsteps immediately alerted Fenella who, in one lithe, sinuous movement, glided off the sofa and across the room to hide between an armchair and the piano, knowing that we would in all probability, cross in front of her and go into the kitchen. With eyes bright and whiskers twitching she crouched, in pleasurable anticipation, from time to time peeping out from behind the chair and drawing back again, completely unaware that the rest of her quivering backside and flickering tail were definitely in view.

There were three courses open to the 'intended victim'; we could either run the gauntlet and be tripped up by the all-embracing paws, or we could call for assistance from anyone in the kitchen - who would arrive carrying a large tea-tray which they rattled in front of her just as she was about to pounce. This usually confused her and distracted her attention. The last method, generally adopted, was to quietly slip out of the front door at the bottom of the stairs, run round the house, and re-enter by the back door, leaving Fenella to wait in vain.

Tigers, like domestic cats, are compulsive claw sharpeners. They claw at trees to pull off the old horny flakes from which emerge the new sharp, curved claws. Great satisfaction seems to be gained from this exercise, and Fenella was no exception. When she was confined to the hut, she sharpened her claws on the wooden floor planks, but now she was in the house she obviously had other ideas. My mother was far from happy when the two adjoining sides of a built-out cupboard became Fenny's claw sharpening post. As the practice continued, Mother complained that not only would there be no paint on the doors, but soon there would not even be any doors. To this day the cupboard, with its deeply grooved claw marks, remains as a proud reminder that Fenella, the housetrained tigress, had sharpened her claws there.

As Fenella had always accompanied us in South Africa, it seemed natural that we should take her for walks in the neighbouring countryside - especially as she needed plenty of exercise. We always went in the same direction - along the quiet, narrow drystone walled lanes, up the hill, and into the woods and moors beyond. We never took Fenella along the busy streets of Holmfirth.

Fenella enjoyed these daily excursions immensely. For the first half mile she led the way, striding forward with briskness and pulling strongly on her lead, eventually her pace became slower as she ambled behind, deciding finally to sit down and look around.

Fenella loved meeting people and was friendly to all humans. I always felt that she identified herself as another person. Although some passers-by kept well away from her, others stopped and stroked her. Children in particular were never afraid of her and often followed behind, stroking her back, but I always warned them to keep well at the rear to avoid getting in her way or under her feet, in case she accidentally tripped them up.

Fenella especially loved to wander off the tarmac road and on to the soft grass in the fields and woods. As the wind blew through her whiskers, and the long grass and bracken swished against her sides, she prowled along, happy to be in her natural surroundings.

It is strange that any hazards encountered on these walks concerned other animals, not people. The sweet, heavy smell of cows grazing in the fields stopped Fenella in her tracks. Whilst usually the cows were on the other side of the wall where she could not see them, their wafting scent tantalised her, causing the young tiger to mill excitedly about, or to sit down where she was and savour the smell. Naturally, we often met dogs, and their attitude towards Fenella varied considerably. Some dogs sniffed at her in a friendly way, whilst others lay flat, trying to make themselves invisible. Strangely, big dogs were horrified - their hackles rose and they stopped dead in their tracks, then they turned swiftly, running and yelping into the distance. The real problem came from small, yapping dogs, which darted unwittingly under a garden gate. There was one in particular, a gallant little Cairn terrier named Shandy, who seemed to sense when we were about. Barking shrilly, he would endeavour to scramble through the six inches of space beneath the gate. One day, as we passed, the gate was open, and suddenly Shandy hurtled out, dancing around Fenella with defiance and barking at the top of his voice. Fenella, not accustomed to this unfriendly behaviour, turned swiftly and swiped a paw at the dog. I was terrified of an accident and intervened even more quickly with my wellington-clad leg - which was badly bruised as a result. Fortunately the dog ran away unhurt.

One of our most singular encounters was with a large brown carthorse which belonged to a farmer higher up the road. Fenella was fascinated by the horse, who in turn was intrigued by the tigress. It was as though some strange telepathic communication existed between them, for even when the cart-horse was two fields away and unable to see Fenella as we passed along the road, it would immediately stop grazing, toss its head as though it had received a signal, clump through the fields, and look benevolently over the wall. Fenella used to sit down in the road and look at the horse with rapture, her chin wobbling a little as she uttered inaudible mews. I always held Fenella's chain tightly to prevent her getting too near to the horse. I could never understand the attraction between these two animals, if attraction it could be called, as the big lumbering carthorse stood solidly, blinking sleepily, its thick bottom lip drooping, until Fenella had gazed her fill and reluctantly decided to move further up the road.

Our next task was to accustom Fenny to riding in our car. She had travelled in cars before when we were in South Africa, but then she had been small enough to be carried in my lap. This time it was different, she was so much larger now and would have to step into the car of her own accord. Our 'elderly' Austin twelve had a roomy back seat - at least it was roomy to us — but I wondered what Fenella would think of it.

I led her down the garden steps and on to the road. Fenella quite obviously imagined this was the start of her usual walk, until she was suddenly confronted with the open door of the car. Cautiously, she placed a paw on the running-board and peered curiously into the interior. Suddenly she back-pedalled hastily. Was this some new type of cage? If so, she didn't intend to be caught again.

Once again the butter ration solved the problem. At that time I think Fenny had most of the butter ration. How hard it is to imagine today that in those times we received two ounces per person per week. Very slowly, aided by the tempting morsel, Fenella was gently coaxed to climb inside again, then her long tail was equally carefully tucked in with her. Quickly and quietly I shut the door, and while I was still plying her generously with butter, my father eased the car forwards.

After my father had driven a couple of miles up the hill, we arrived at a quiet, sandy moorland lane; here, car training commenced in earnest. I pushed both back doors wide open and proceeded to lead her through the car. In we went at one door and out at the other, to assure her that there was nothing to be afraid of. Fenella really was a most intelligent animal and amazingly soon she had learnt the new lesson. From then onwards, Fenella really enjoyed travelling in the car; sometimes she sat with her rear on the seat, her paws on the floor and rested her chin on the back of the front seat; sometimes she rested her chin on my father's shoulder as he drove the car. Usually she reclined comfortably on the back seat, looking a picture of ease and pride. She loved this mode of travel so much that whenever she saw the car, she used to wait by the closed doors, hoping someone would open them for her. We, too, were very pleased and regarded this as one of Fenella's most useful achievements as it enabled her to travel with us on many outings which otherwise would not have been possible.

Fenella in the garden

8

We take Fenella to Blackpool

For the next six months, Fenella lived the life of an over-sized kitten, spending most of the day in the house with the family. Each evening she was banished to the hut in which she had spent her quarantine.

Our grey stone house was high up on the hillside and above the village, beyond the back garden were open fields rising to the ridge of a hill. Fortunately not many people passed along the road, and with wartime fuel rationing hardly any cars came up the hill. Therefore we could usually walk Fenny up the hill and along the country lanes and farm tracks without arousing undue comment. Pupils from the nearby school had been among the first to come and look at the young tigress but the novelty soon wore off. Whilst they would eagerly congregate round her if she was in the vicinity, they no longer came to the house to plague us for a view of Fenny.

Fenella was then appreciably bigger and had almost reached her full height. The ruff which had appeared round her face was thick and silky, she was also losing her fluffy fur and becoming quite sleek. Her behaviour was more restrained and she no longer regarded Meg and myself as permanent sparring partners. Fenella's newly-acquired dignified manner revealed her as a very ladylike tiger who moved both gracefully and majestically. I couldn't help but feel proud of this elegant and beautifully marked creature who loped effortlessly along at my side, the tip of her tail held in a delicate upward curve.

Fenella was always conscious of the difference between walking while attached to a lead, and being allowed to run free in a field or wood. The change in her gait was instantaneous. On the lead she padded quietly at my side with an easy, loping stride, satisfied to travel at my speed. In a field, freed from the lead, she moved sinuously and stealthily with silent purpose. When led down a woodland slope she slithered, brushed against bushes and seemed clumsy; free, and engaged in stalking, she moved down the same slope without moving either a leaf or a twig in silent controlled grace.

When playing in a field, Fenny was probably at her best and most natural. You had only to come up behind her, clap your hands, and she leapt up into the air, turning as though airborne, and gave chase. This continued until you were exhausted or until she caught and floored her opponent. Then she wrestled with her prey, gripping her victim in her huge paws. Though her claws might catch in your clothing, they were never exposed sufficiently to catch the flesh underneath, which she could so easily have done. To her, the whole affair was a huge wrestling game which she enjoyed immensely. Once her claws were fastened in your clothing it was far from easy to get her to release her grip. The only way was to tickle the pads of her feet which made her retract her claws while you slipped out of her grasp. Sometimes she locked her fangs about my forearm, then I had to insert a finger of the other hand and tickle the roof of her mouth so that she would open her jaws and release my arm. This may seem an unorthodox method of freeing yourself from the grip of a fully grown tiger, and it is not one that I can recommend to a normal wild animal trainer. Not many wild animals would allow you to tickle their feet, or insert a finger in their mouth without nipping it off between their very powerful incisors.

It soon became obvious to us how expensive it is to feed a fully-grown tiger on horsemeat 'fit for human consumption', and this was the only kind of meat that Fenella liked. But we also began to realise that we possessed a unique animal, a perfectly tame and domesticated tigress, and it seemed to us that there must be many people eager to see such a rarity. Perhaps we could help to keep the 'wolf' from the door by putting our exceptional pet on show.

In order to exhibit an animal in a show, you first have to register it under the performing Animals (Regulation) Act, even though no tricks are performed by the animal. On the form we described Fenella as: 'A domesticated tiger, having been brought up from birth in the household, and showing its tameness and what can be accomplished by kindness.'

Next, we had to find a theatrical agent. During the war many agents found bases in safer areas away from London and the entertainment mecca of wartime seemed to be Blackpool, where there was also a large RAF training centre. So we packed quickly, put Fenella into our caravan trailer, and towed her en route for Blackpool.

Fenella seemed to accept this mode of travel, much as she accepted everything else. If we were with her then everything was all right. She was a little surprised when the caravan rumbled off on its journey and braced her legs against the uneven motion, gazing at the floor in wonderment; the swishing of the tyres disconcerted her also. I talked to her softly, trying to soothe her ruffled nerves. Soon her anxiety went and she curled up on the settee bed at my side, whilst I continued to stroke her. She had, after all, spent her earliest years being shunted backwards and forwards in a coach on South African railways, and probably thought this was just another peculiar way that her parents travelled. She was, as I have said before, convinced that we were her parents, and that she was merely a different shaped human being.

On one occasion, at Belle Vue Zoo, Manchester, I walked Fenella past a cage containing three tiger cubs and paused to see their reactions. One cub, who was ill, completely ignored her; the second chuckled at her, giving the 'snuffling' sound we had learned to identify as affection in Fenella; the third cub spat at Fenny, It was obvious they recognised our tigress as one of them, but Fenella only stared at them curiously and continued on her way - clearly she did not identify herself with them.

To return to Blackpool. Apart from the blackout, this gay city, crowded with servicemen and holiday makers, seemed far removed from the war. Theatres and cinemas were open, and giant ballrooms - throbbing with the music of famous bands - were packed with enthusiastic dancers. People queued along the 'Golden Mile' to stare with disbelief at the oddities hidden in dingy booths.

On the outskirts of the town we found a friendly farmer, who allowed us to camp in his fields, dotted with rows of golden haycocks; between the dividing hedges of hawthorn, elder and bramble shimmered a pool of water. It was a hot summer's day, and my father took little persuading to park the caravan by this inviting spot.

My parents then began a tour of theatrical agents' offices, but none of them seemed interested in presenting a tame tigress in any of their shows. Their stock question was, "Where can I see you work?" It was a real chicken and egg situation. How can you get work in the theatre if no agent will book you until he has seen you working in the theatre?

We did, however, find a small amusement park on the cliffs at Clevelys, to the north of Blackpool. On this site, amidst the children's roundabouts, hoopla stalls, rifle ranges and other attractions, I noticed a sideshow exhibiting a five-legged sheep. Nearby we met an old acquaintance who was showing his performing dogs in a booth. "Why don't you show your tiger here?" he suggested. "There's plenty of room, so make yourself a few bob." It wasn't at all what we had in mind and were ill-equipped for such a venture, but decided to give it a trial.

We obtained some white card and in large black letters my father wrote:

'FENELLA, THE DOMESTICATED TIGRESS'
Adults 3d, Children 2d.'

At that time you could see the entire stock of animals in the Tower Menagerie for only one shilling, so we considered 3d for adults a reasonable charge to see one tame tigress. A box was placed in front of the caravan to use as a platform, and we fastened some photos of Fenny outside the caravan - we were in business.

Feeling rather nervous, I stood in the doorway of the caravan waiting for the rush of people who, I expected, would be keen to see the tiger, but was soon astounded how little impact our outfit made on the passing populace. Most people hurried straight past us, heading for the beach.

One or two people ambled over to the caravan and looked at our notice and photographs, but that was all. Eventually one small boy tugged persistently on his mother's arm and persuaded her, against her will, to pay the fee that allowed them to stand and look over the half-door into the van. The boy was delighted with the sight of a real live tiger sitting on the settee in the caravan, but his mother was more than taken aback. "Ee! I didn't expect it to be a live 'un," she confided, "I thought it would be stuffed!"

Slowly, others came and parted with their coins. Many obviously expected a hoax and were delighted when they found it was the real thing. People were fascinated to find that they could lean over the door and actually touch the beautiful striped flanks of Fenny as she walked to and fro along the caravan floor. It was noticeable that children were far less afraid of her than were adults. A child needed no encouraging to lean over and stroke what, to them, may well have seemed a huge pussy cat, but their parents were often very reluctant to follow the example of their offspring.

One Lancastrian who saw Fenella lying on the settee beside me said, "I'll bet she wouldn't let anyone touch you," then added, "Yes, I bet if anyone attacked you, she wouldn't half go for them." He seemed satisfied with his conclusions as he finally remarked, "Yes, you've got a right protector there." He sounded so pleased about it that I didn't like to disillusion him by saying that as she was a cat, she probably wouldn't bother unless the attacker also turned on her.

I was greatly amused to find that quite a number of women, on seeing the caravan with its discreet leaded windows and gay curtains, would cautiously approach the caravan door and ask how much I charged to tell fortunes. I began to feel like the original Gypsy Rose Lee. What a pity I wasn't a clairvoyant, I thought - business would have been so much better.

Then there were the young men who came to look at the tigress but stayed on to 'chat up' the girl who was looking after Fenella. With such limited room on the platform, these would-be admirers obstructed the admittance of other customers, as they stayed on and on, unsuccessfully trying to date me.

One day I wandered over to the booth housing the five-legged sheep. The showman, a thin-faced man, wearing a black bowler hat, yellow checked waistcoat and riding breeches, was expounding the freakishness of his five-legged beast to a small gathering who were listening half-heartedly. The man wanted a 'gee' to ginger the group into activity. Recognising me as being 'in the business', the man gave me a wink and a nod, and I marched boldly into the booth. Almost immediately the undecided, who had their decision made for them, followed me unhesitatingly into the tent. I wondered who were the real sheep, the group who blindly followed a leader, or the one on display in the tent.

I was intrigued to see the sheep. In my ignorance I had imagined a fifth limb growing out of its body, but it proved to be an appendix growing from one of its hind legs and standing out at a slight angle.

Afterwards, I asked the showman, "How's business?" He shrugged his shoulders, "A bit quiet now but it'll buck up come Wakes Week." We never found out if business justified his optimism, for by then we had abandoned Blackpool in search of more lucrative pastures.

Whilst in Blackpool the highlight of Fenella's days were the mornings. We took her out in the field where she was intrigued by the haycocks. She scrambled awkwardly to the top of them, as they were an insecure perch for such a large animal, and then slid down to the ground with delirious abandon. This she repeated several times before resuming her walk around the field.

At first it proved difficult to induce Fenella to return to the caravan for she greatly enjoyed her freedom. It is never easy to get a recalcitrant tiger to do anything it doesn't want to. It cannot be physically forced, as it is as strong as the normal human and almost as heavy. The only remedy was by gentle persuasion. We never found or considered any alternative method.

When Fenella was confronted with the open caravan door she knew quite well that she was intended to go back in there, but if she shied away from the door - dug in her heels and refused to go further - the only thing to do was to take her for another walk round the field and try again. I might have to walk her several times to the door and she might still refuse to enter, so that I would have to persist and continue walking until she agreed to enter. It was always easier when there were two people trying to get her inside, as one could offer her a titbit to lure her inside and the other could keep a firm hold on her lead.

One day, whilst I was trying to coax her back into the caravan, she backed away so smartly and with such incredible speed, that she slipped backwards into a pool of stagnant water nearby, where she floundered about and then emerged covered with green slime and chickweed. She looked such a chastened and subdued tiger, who obviously felt very sorry for herself, that I was compelled to laugh. The laugh, however, was on me, as I had to dry and clean her of the evil-smelling slime which coated her beautiful fur. After about a week the charm of the field must have worn off, because she began to agree to return to the caravan quite amiably.

On another occasion, I was alone with Fenny in the caravan; she was lying, as she preferred, on the bed-settee. Not for Fenella a hard floor when there was an upholstered, comfortable couch just the right length for her. Through the opened top-half of the door, the sun was shining brightly on her golden flanks. Her amber eyes were narrow slits of contentment and she would now and again lazily wash a paw. Doubtless she would have washed me also had I been sitting with her, for she was never averse to giving her companion an occasional rub over in between doing her own toilet. From a nearby hedge came the chirruping of contesting sparrows and closer still familiar crooning, clucking sounds which were so familiar to me that I failed to recognise their significance. But the sounds were not familiar to Fenella. Suddenly she was alert. With an effortless movement she rose to her feet, poised for a second with her front paws on the top half of the door, surveyed the scene and, in a flash, she was gone.

There was an immediate uproar outside the van. Hens screeched, squawked and cackled, scattering in all directions desperately trying to get off the ground by frantically beating the air with their wings. In the midst of this uproar Fenny stood poised, looking as surprised as the hens, who had been quietly pecking crumbs by the caravan door when suddenly a tigress descended on them from the heavens above. No wonder they were scared and dashed away in a mad panic. Fenella clearly thought that this was a new game, designed to amuse her, and entered into the spirit of it immediately. Choosing the nearest fowl she loped gaily after it, pausing to give it occasional playful swipes with her forepaw, as the screeching demented bird fled towards the hedge.

I shot out of the caravan and started to chase the tiger, yelling at the top of my voice, "Come back, Fenny", and "Stop it!" all to no avail for she was thoroughly enjoying the display put on especially for her. Chasing after her, I got near enough to catch her by the tail and, although this didn't stop her, it did at least slow her down. Across the field we proceeded in this curious procession a terrified, squawking bundle of feathers, followed by a loping tigress who was dragging a young blonde lady clutching the tiger's tail. Eventually the wretched bird reached the hedge. With a prodigious whirring of feathers and a final high pitched cackle of relief it struggled to safety over the hedge.

Completely baffled by the disappearance of her new plaything, Fenny snuffled and hunted round the bottom of the hedge for some time before condescending to be taken back to the caravan, delighted with the entertainment, but sorry that it had been of such short duration. Luckily, none of the hens were hurt, as they might well have been if Fenella had really grabbed one of them, but I am certain that the farmer had one hen whose mind was on other things for the next day or so.

Business at Blackpool, as I have already remarked, was far from good, particularly as we could only show Fenella to two people at a time, standing on the box platform at our caravan door. They wanted to know her history and a host of other questions, not always related to wild animal training, such as, "What are you doing tonight?" I decided it was a laborious and slow way of earning a livelihood. At the end of each day we totted up our takings, eight shillings, twelve shillings and at the weekend, possibly one pound. If it rained we earned nothing.

In addition there was the worrying business of obtaining fresh meat. As we were unable to find a horsemeat shop for human consumption in the area, we were forced to obtain meat from horse slaughterers and knackers' yards. To show that it was unfit for human consumption, this meat was liberally stained with green dye. Often it was of such poor quality that Fenella refused to touch it, making us wonder what the animal had died from. We pooled our meat ration and gave it to Fenny, but as this only amounted to a couple of mouthfuls to her it was small comfort to a hungry tiger. To supplement the meagre diet we gave her porridge made from oats and cooked in milk.

After three weeks we decided that it was time to sink our losses and return home. At least there was a human consumption horsemeat shop in Huddersfield. Shortly after returning home, and whilst taking Fenella for a walk along one of our country lanes, I encountered a stranger who stopped and showed great interest in this obviously tame and very beautiful tiger, who allowed herself to be led by a young blonde lady. He stroked her back, hesitantly at first, then more boldly. "What a lovely animal", he remarked. "Do you know, I've just been on holiday to Blackpool where I saw a five-legged sheep in a side-show. I reckon you ought to take Fenella there and show her. You'd make yourselves a fortune."

9

Trouble with the Council

Perhaps it was inevitable that Fenella should fall foul of the local council which, by its very nature, tends to be suspicious of the unorthodox; and what could be more unorthodox than having a tiger as a household pet? A certain section of our Urban District Council became convinced that Fenny was a menace to the community, and even felt convinced that one day a lone plane would drop a bomb on our particular house in Holmfirth, destroying it and releasing a crazed tiger, who would maul and slay most of the panic-stricken villagers.

This began, I suppose, the day Fenella stopped a funeral!

The lane past our house, besides leading to fields and moors, led also to the cemetery of the parish church; a little distance from the cemetery was the field in which Fenella's favourite horse grazed.

Snarling

On this particular day, Fenella was out for a stroll with my sister Meg, and had just reached the field with the horse who, keen-eyed as ever, cantered down from the top of the meadow to put his head over the wall and admire his old acquaintance. Fenny, never one to be discourteous, stopped to greet her friend, and sat down in the middle of the road. At this precise moment, the cortège hove into view and there, in the middle of the narrow, fourteen-foot wide road, between blackened stone walls, they saw the imperial figure of a tiger. The hearse came to an abrupt stop, so did the first car containing the chief mourners, then the second car stopped.

Meg, anxious at this unexpected situation, tried to coax Fenny to her feet, but it was the tiger's practice to look lovingly and long at her friend the horse, who in turn drooled with pleasure from thick black lips at the sight of her. It was clear that while the tiger occupied the centre of the road, the cortège was unable to pass.

Since Fenella was reluctant to leave the spot, Meg tried to spur her into action by giving a sharp tug on the chain that served as a lead. Fenny, resenting this unfriendly behaviour, pawed out at Meg, and in doing so, one of her claws caught in a link of her chain. This presented a further problem and poor Meg, becoming more and more embarrassed, had to bend down and slowly extricate the claw from the chain. This achieved, Fenella - who seemed to attribute the whole matter to my sister's carelessness - sought to chastise her yet again with an outstretched paw. As Meg was still bending down, her paw this time caught Meg's shoulder and became embedded in her ancient tweed jacket which was not up to such treatment. The fabric tore slightly and Fenny's claw was caught again, this time in the white woollen cardigan worn under the jacket. Almost immediately, a long loop of white wool emerged through the rip, still entangled in Fenny's claw. As quickly as she could, Meg undid the loop of wool, wondering what on earth could happen next. She rose to her feet and spoke much more harshly than usual to the tiger, who now seemed quite surprised at what she had done. So surprised was Fenella, that she forgot about the horse and her determination to remain in the road, and allowed herself to be led, unprotesting, past the hearse, the cortège, and the surprised mourners.

Had it been a herd of cows or a flock of sheep that had obstructed the road and stopped a funeral, it would not have been noteworthy, but a tiger on a lead is news! The reporter assigned to cover the funeral hardly expected such good fortune. The next week the local weekly newspaper carried banner headlines, TIGER STOPS FUNERAL! This was only the beginning. Three days later, I was glancing through our front window, when I saw a car stop outside the house, then other cars drew up and several men got out. They seemed to be conferring with each other and looking upwards at the house. Eventually they formed themselves into a united group and started to ascend the steps alongside the garden. I noticed that some of them carried expensive camera equipment, and suddenly it dawned on me who the visitors were.

"Hey!" I yelled to the family, who were just finishing breakfast, "I think we're being invaded by the press." They were, indeed, reporters and cameramen from the national press.

Unknown to us, the previous evening the local council had debated the matter of the tiger - whether it should be allowed to be led through the streets, and, whether it had any right at all to exist in their midst.

"People are afraid," stated one councillor, although this sweeping statement was never confirmed by the populace at large. "The tiger must be stopped," was the considered opinion of another worthy. "They lead it round on a bit of string," was yet another profound and wholly untrue declaration in the council chamber. "It even held up a funeral the other day," seemed the only authentic declaration made that night, but the whole meeting was dismissed by one of the city papers in their morning edition, with a headline reading:

> TIGER, ON A BIT OF STRING,
> WALKS STREETS.

This startling headline had been seized upon by the national press, resulting in the appearance of press reporters and photographers outside the house, sent to investigate the authenticity of the story.

My father's attitude was predictable. He was outraged by this invasion of his privacy and flatly refused to let them take any pictures. We certainly did not want the kind of publicity which made our tigress the centre of controversy. But the press were persistent. I suppose persistence is a virtue in their trade, and some of them dare not have gone back to face irate editors without some kind of story.

They hung around most of the morning. They asked questions. They sought to badger us, then, when that didn't succeed, they tried wheedling and coaxing. It became clear that they were going to camp outside the house until they got what they had come for.

Eventually, much to my surprise, my father had a sudden change of heart. Maybe he thought, "If you can't beat 'em then join 'em."

It was almost noon, and time for the local school to close for lunch. My father turned to the reporters,

"In a few minutes the children will be coming home from school for their dinners. You can take some pictures of Fenny with the children."

He looked at the disbelieving newsmen and smiled,

"If she eats one of them, you'll be able to take a picture of that as well!"

I put the chain round Fenny's neck and we led her along the road to meet the schoolchildren, who greeted her rapturously. There must have been many a child late home for lunch that day, who related excitedly to their parents how they had walked up and down the road, stroking the tiger, while photographers ran ahead taking pictures from all angles.

It was odd how these pressmen, initially rather timid and not too keen to be too near to our tiger, found courage when they saw how fearlessly the small children greeted her, stroked her, and how much Fenny obviously enjoyed their attentions. Of all those present that day, certainly the most dignified was the tigress, for the pressmen pushed and struggled to get the best angles for pictures, and the children, showing off and wanting to see themselves in at least one of the hundreds of pictures taken that day, pushed and jostled for star positions.

Afterwards, when the children had gone home, we returned to the house with Fenella, sat her on the settee, and I curled up beside her while the photographers blazed away, taking shot after shot of film.

In many of the photographs taken that day (and which we still have) poor Fenny looks slightly dazed by it all. I think she found the popping of the bright flash bulbs rather surprising. Had she not been a very friendly and amiable tiger, she would probably have shown her feelings for the inconsiderate pressmen by nipping one or two of them rather smartly. That would have made a bigger press story, but I feel sure that the pictures taken by the national press that day proved, beyond any doubt, what a storm in a tea-cup had been raised by the local council.

The next day, matters became more hectic. I suppose there were a large proportion of local residents who, if vaguely aware that someone had a tiger in the Holmfirth district, had thought nothing at all about it. That day, every daily paper carried stories of Holmfirth's tame tiger and had pictures of her in the midst of happy, carefree schoolchildren.

These stories in the national press brought home the fact to many local people who previously had been quite unaware of the tiger's presence, that there was something unusual to see if they took the trouble to go and look.

And come they did, in their droves, tramping up our garden steps, knocking at the door at all times of the day and night, anxious to see the celebrated tiger that had made a headline in their daily paper that morning.

Fenella - always on her best behaviour on such occasions, seemed to enjoy being admired by humans. She paraded before them with a calm aloof detachment, graciously permitting them to stroke her beautiful striped coat.

The Entertainments Officer of the Royal Corps of Signals - the troops garrisoned in and around the Huddersfield area - was not slow to catch on to the attraction of a tame tigress. He was staging a concert for the general public at the Huddersfield Palace Theatre the following Sunday, and Fenny was invited to make a guest appearance. I walked Fenella onto the stage; she seemed quite unconcerned by the noise of the band, the bright stage lighting and the general strangeness of the professional stage. She didn't do much. She didn't have to. Soldiers came up from the body of the theatre to stroke her. Everyone was thrilled and excited; nothing like her had ever been seen before and she was, I must repeat it, an extremely handsome animal. It was also very obvious that she was a real 'trouper', a creature who takes to the theatre as naturally as a duck takes to water.

But the council had not finished. It seems that they had already embarked on a course of action which I think, in all fairness, would not have been decided upon if the neutral members of the council had had the benefit of the national press features at an earlier stage. They had, however, solemnly agreed to have a special meeting to consider the matter of the HOLMFIRTH TIGER, and to decide on the best method of keeping her off the streets and safeguarding the health of their electorate.

I was horrified at the idea of this meeting. We didn't know what it would imply and where it could lead. We had no idea of the power of the local authority in such cases. Could they force us to part with Fenny? This was unthinkable. Maybe we would be forced to have her in a zoo, and this was unthinkable too. She was not a wild animal; she was a happy, contented and very amiable big cat, who was very fond of us and liked people. After all, she had never known anything but kindness from humans; they had been her parents and fed her from birth. She looked to us for warmth, affection and companionship, as well as continual supply of food.

She had never hurt anyone and was unlikely to deliberately do so. We had never met anyone who was afraid of her, usually quite the contrary. Some adults, on seeing her for the first time, were a little apprehensive, since they had been conditioned to believe that tigers are the most cruel and ferocious of all jungle creatures. But soon they would overcome their misgivings and pluck up sufficient courage to stroke this very friendly animal.

We had never taken her into the streets of Holmfirth, but only walked her along the country lanes on the hillside above the village. As for the 'piece of string', the story which had delighted the newspapermen, this was arrant nonsense. "Anyone who can't tell the difference between a steel chain and a bit of string should have his eyes tested," snorted my father.

During all this time we were never approached by the disgruntled councillors themselves. None of them, to the best of my knowledge, ever bothered to come and see the tiger 'that rankled their bosoms'. Pressmen came and went and, on the whole, since they presented the truth of the matter, proved to be our best advocates.

The postmen, too, would have been competent authorities to judge. They visited our house daily, bearing an ever-increasing load of letters, and none of them seemed in the least reluctant to visit 'the tiger's lair'.

The letters which flooded in to us showed that Fenella had far more friends than enemies. Many correspondents were concerned that we might have to destroy our pet, and begged us not to allow this, others offered to take her as a pet into their own homes. Several zoos wrote informing us of a comfortable cage they could provide, and of a suitable mate that was just pining for her company. Circus proprietors wanted to buy her and one even offered us a pair of lion cubs in part exchange. But the majority of the mail was from ordinary people who wished us well, many asking politely if it would be possible for them to come and see Fenny.

We received only one letter of abuse from a writer who stated that, in his opinion, both the owner and the tiger should be behind bars!

My mother was the first to open the morning paper containing a report of the special council meeting to 'ban the tiger'. With bated breath, we listened, as she read the forthright and shattering pronouncements of our elected representatives.

"We must kick the tiger out," announced one worthy.

"It is a public danger," stated another.

"It should be a police matter," said a third.

"What are the police doing?" demanded another angrily.

"We have a vicious animal at large in our midst. This was reported to the police a week ago. What have they done about it? "

It was at this point, I think, that one of the less excitable councillors pointed out that in Britain, even in wartime, laws must be broken before the police can act. Fenella had broken no laws, merely outraged a number of preconceived ideas.

The most surprising statement came from the member who urged, "Prompt action should be taken. I understand this animal might have cubs in the spring. Then . . . " he announced triumphantly, "we'll have a whole street full of tigers!"

"Cubs!" Meg was highly indignant. "He must think Fenny has been out on the tiles!"

It next transpired that after their rantings and tub-thumpings, the worthy councillors had turned the matter over to their lawyers, to instruct us to keep the animal under proper control.

"She is under proper control," replied my father wearily, and began to talk darkly about not being wanted in Holmfirth, and that there were other places we could go to live.

The 'tiger legends' were not without humour, and some of the stories in the newspapers relied on inventive imagination rather than accuracy. One myth, oft quoted, was of the soldier stationed at Holmfirth, who fell asleep one summer in the long grass and woke to find a tiger staring down on him. Terrified, he jumped up and raced back to his billet where, white and trembling, he related his rude awakening to his incredulous comrades in arms who thought he had gone mad. His C.O., who knew that tigers don't roam the hillsides of Pennine villages, clapped the fellow in irons and confined him to the barracks. Then he found, to his horror, that Holmfirth really did have a tiger and the incarcerated fusilier was freed with alacrity.

It never happened, of course, but when fantasy is so much better than truth, who cares whether or not it was fiction? It could have happened, and maybe it took our minds off the war at a period when we weren't doing very well.

Various American newspapers published stories of Fenella's exploits and they were frequently even further from the truth than the soldier in the grass.

One headline reads:

PET TIGER TAKES SPOTLIGHT FROM WAR IN ENGLAND

We had to laugh when we read how the citizens of Holmfirth, stumbling along in the gloom of the blackout, were terrified when they smelled pungent jungle smells and saw wild eyes glinting out of the darkness whilst sinuous, furry flanks slid past their legs.

Now we began to have letters from people who wanted one of the cubs that our tiger was to produce in the spring. Five young men at Brown University, Providence, U.S.A. wrote asking if they could have a cub as a pet for their dormitory.

Unfortunately for the anti-tiger lobby in the council, their feelings were not shared by the constabulary. Our local inspector, a bluff and happy Cumbrian, who had served his time in the police force but was retained due to the wartime emergency, frequently brought friends and members of the C.I.D. to see Fenny. His favourite ploy was to ruffle her fur, pull on her whiskers, and declare she was as harmless as an old tabby cat. Little did he know that the tiger didn't relish these attentions. We, who had watched her grow up, knew that pricked ears and a twitching tail meant that she was not enchanted with having her whiskers pulled, and she preferred her fur to be stroked, not ruffled. Fenella was capable on occasions of dislike, and could summon a most tigerish snarl, with narrowed eyes and bared fangs, warning the offender that enough was enough.

Mercifully, she never betrayed her resentment to others, confining her spleen to members of the family, so the Inspector never knew that the 'old tabby cat' could become a savage tiger, if sufficiently provoked.

The local police, when questioned by the press, replied that they had never had any complaints; and one officer, who covered our area, remarked that he took no more notice of her than of a large dog.

Maybe the constabulary didn't take much account of our tiger, but one of their number, a comparative newcomer to the district, took more than a little notice of my sister Meg. He seemed to succeed where other suitors had failed. I expect it was a case of 'Love me, love my tiger!' but soon we were having a wedding in the family.

The police officer later confessed that the first occasion he visited our house was with some trepidation, for he was a coward at heart. It was late evening and Fenny was asleep in the kitchen, whilst he was received in the front room. Because it was late and Fenny was tired, she did not follow her usual habit of getting up and going to inspect the visitor, smelling at him and deciding whether she liked him or not. He was not, on that first visit, confronted with the tiger, otherwise he feels pretty sure that it would have ruined a wonderful romance. Ultimately he became quite fond of Fenella, but Meg was his main interest. Fenny seemed to tolerate him fairly well; my sister tolerated him far better.

**Meg's husband Dex with Fenella.
Meeting local schoolchildren**

10

Fenella — In 'Show Business'

In retrospect I can only suppose that the numerous stories and photographs in the national press, particularly those portraying Fenella walking in the country lanes surrounded by a crowd of children, proved to be the best advertisements we could have wished for. Overnight, Fenny had become a nationally known animal, and her continued existence as a household pet was almost a cause célèbre.

This massive publicity came at a time when the news on all battlefronts was universally bad and, as a consequence, the national press found the story a welcome change from the gloom that attended most of their headlines.

As a result of this 'sudden fame', we were approached by the management of the annual Christmas circus at Belle Vue, Manchester, to show her as a star attraction at their forthcoming production. This was wonderful - precisely what we needed. Show business was our profession; Fenella had to be fed, so it was natural that we should look to the entertainments' industry to find the wherewithal to feed our growing pet tigress.

But there was one great problem. We had no act in the known sense. Besides lacking a 'known act', we had not even got a performer, if one considered the talents of our star turn. All we had was an amiable tigress who liked human beings, was happy to be led into their midst, and who enjoyed the friendship of local children who patted and stroked her.

Fenella might be persuaded to do things of which she approved, like chasing a ball, springing on some moving object, as a kitten will pounce on a ball of wool, but then - on the other hand - she might not. It all depended on how the young tigress felt at the particular time. She would condescend to play with us if she were feeling kittenish, but if she felt it was time for her to lie down and have a rest, she would do so. We were dealing with an unpredictable element in whom we had great faith, but whose experience as a performer - to say the least of it - was somewhat limited.

We did realise, however, that whilst we often took Fenella for granted, she was, at that time, unique in the history of wild animal training. I have often wondered whether the management of the Belle

Vue amusement park were far-sighted and shrewd when they engaged our tigress to appear in their circus, and whether they fully appreciated the implications of what they were doing - they were engaging a 'supposedly' tame tiger to appear in a circus ring without cage or bars. Perhaps they merely felt we were a heaven-sent stop-gap to put on in place of the normal cage full of wild, growling animals that were, during the hostilities, banned from such centres of entertainment, due to the danger of them becoming freed through air-raids or enemy action, and attacking and savaging members of the public.

Throughout Fenella's life, despite her continued amiability, it was the solemn and considered opinion of all authorities on the training of wild animals that one day the tigress would 'turn on us!' I remember how various circus proprietors, eager to see this phenomenon, used to visit our caravan and stand anxiously at the door, staring doubtfully at the tigress. They were always extremely reluctant to step into the same confines as Fenella, because, I suppose, their knowledge of tigers and lions never allowed them to feel safe without stout bars and a weapon for protection.

"Do you mean to say you can actually take her meat away from her?" asked one incredulously, clearly indicating that one day he expected us to be torn to pieces if we continued to act in such a foolish way. And yet, when Fenella's portion of meat was being cut from the giant hunk kept in the refrigerator, if she thought we weren't watching, she might seize the whole piece and carry it away triumphantly to her allocated dining space, but when we retrieved it she usually surrendered it gracefully. I suppose she was conditioned to believe that food only came from one source, that it never failed to arrive, and, possibly, that humans knew what was good for her.

When we were first approached by the management of Belle Vue, we warned them that Fenella was not a performing animal, and that she could not do tricks - such as walking planks, riding giant balls - at a word of command, although sometimes, if she felt like it, she was able to do some of these feats which are inherently easy to feline animals. The management were quite satisfied with this arrangement and confirmed that they didn't want her to do anything. They thought it would prove to be a sufficient novelty to have an uncaged tigress in a circus ring, especially if one or two children could be safely invited into the ring to stroke her. This would be something never seen before, and would more than delight the audience. The management were fully aware of the publicity Fenella had received and were confident that the name of the 'Holmfirth Tiger' on their bills and programmes would in itself be a great attraction.

A couple of days before the circus was due to open, we went over to Belle Vue, at Manchester, taking Fenny in our caravan. Other acts had already arrived and were busy fixing up their apparatus and preparing for the show.

It seemed wonderful to be back in show business, particularly in a circus again, where there always seemed to be a special feeling of closeness and belonging. There are no temperamental singers in a circus, no morose, difficult comedians whose off-stage behaviour contrasts with their comic image. Performers in circuses usually succeed by the sweat of their brows, the racking of their muscles, and the concentrated dedication of trained bodies, in their efforts to achieve balance and grace whilst performing feats at which ordinary men marvel.

As it was wartime, the continental performers were absent from Belle Vue. The Italians and Germans, who have produced great circus artistes, were at war against this country, and their more prudent members had forborne to visit England in the months prior to September 1939. Those who had been performing here found themselves interned under Regulation 18B as enemy aliens, and the English theatre was the poorer thereby. As a consequence, it seemed that almost all the performers at Belle Vue that Christmas were either old friends, or relations of old friends.

We had gone early in order to get Fenny acclimatised to the atmosphere of a circus ring. Although she had been born in a circus, her parents were menagerie animals and not performers. We had taken her, wearing her little harness, into the circus tent between shows, but she had been so young then and I doubted if she would remember. In any case, there is a vast difference between a big top erected on a crossing of baked earth road in Africa, billowing gently in the sub-tropical air, and a large structure like the King's Hall at Belle Vue.

So that she would become accustomed to the feel of the place, we took her several times into the large hall and walked her round the ring, as we were not sure how she would react to these strange surroundings.

Fenella had been quite unimpressed by the bright lights and glare of the theatrical stage at Huddersfield, nor had she been perturbed by the considerable sound of a military dance band blaring forth 'Tiger Rag' with all the gusto that young soldiers' lungs could muster.

We hoped she would be all right in a circus ring, but there were strange smells there, new to her - the smells of performing horses and dogs, also many different sounds - and we wondered how she would react to these. I don't think we were ever seriously perturbed, and I felt quite confident she would behave impeccably as usual, but there was always the uncertainty of strange surroundings. She was a tiger; she had never done this before; no one had ever done this before: The audience would be all around her, tier after tier, rising as far as the eye could see - some of them within a few yards of her, not hidden from view in the dark void that exists beyond the glare of the stage footlights.

Fenella was fascinated with the resilient feel of the coconut fibre ring-mat which she started plucking, digging her sharp claws into it like a playful kitten, and dragging out long tufts of the husky fibre. I had to clap my hands sharply to attract her attention and make her forget the delights of shredding the ring mat.

I was delighted to discover that the tigress had not the slightest objection to mounting on top of the eighteen inch high ring fence and walking along it, allowing herself to be led round its perimeter. This would be something she could do in the 'act' and would make her more clearly visible to the audience. As the time for her debut drew near, I must confess that I felt far more nervous than I would have been doing our accustomed acrobatic routine. It is always something of an ordeal to appear in a new show, especially on the first night in a new town, but to go on a show as a STAR ATTRACTION without having any set routine, or any real idea how any star performer would behave, was even more harrowing than usual.

My mouth felt parched and dry as I began to put my make-up on. Through my mind was passing the same thought, over and over again, "We haven't got an act . . . all I can do is take her into the ring, walk her on the ring fence, and if all goes well, invite one or two children to stroke her . . we haven't got an act." And so it went on. I had to keep reminding myself that while it didn't seem much for a star performer to do, it was more than anyone had done before.

Later on, as we realised what audiences liked to see, we evolved an act that lasted about ten minutes, but on this occasion we only had the bare bones of an idea and an unpredictable tigress.

Fenny was sharing the dressing room with us. At that particular time we hadn't even got a cage or a box in the dressing room in which she could lie down and rest, a place she could regard as home and a safe haven from an unfamiliar environment.

Having no accustomed place in which to lie, Fenella paced restlessly to and fro along the back wall of the dressing-room, exactly as caged wild animals do in zoos and menageries, a trait inherent in wild animals. But Fenella's walking was annoying and distracting to us as we tried to get changed, for the tigress wheeled and turned in our path. The perpetual yapping of a troupe of performing dogs which shared the next dressing room with their trainer was attracting her full attention. The dressing rooms were merely cubicles without any ceiling, and the barking of the dogs over and through the thin partition walls was very close, so no wonder Fenny was excited by their proximity. The tigress would suddenly stop in her perambulations, fix her gaze on some spot on the lower wall, obviously puzzled and baffled by the source of this unaccustomed noise. The clamour reached a crescendo, and Fenella seemed to expect the dogs to break through the partition at any moment.

There were other exciting noises, the sharp clatter of horses' hooves, as the liberty group were brought up from their stable in the cellars under the building. Having a keener smell than humans, the tigress sensed these odours more acutely than we did. Overall was the pervading hum of conversation that precedes a performance, the growth of which made me realise that we should be opening to a full house for our first show.

I had made a ruffle of red net and fashioned a small clown's conical hat with red pom-poms for Fenny to wear in the act, hoping that it would give her a cuddly appearance and allay any fears the audience might have of her. Perhaps the sight of a tiger wearing a ruffle and funny hat might make it seem less dangerous for we were not sure how the public would react to her. Would anxious mothers forbid their offspring to go near such an animal? In which case we would be denied the chance of showing how tame she really was.

Fenella didn't mind the ruffle, but she wasn't keen on the clown's hat. I tried putting it on her head at a jaunty angle but, one quick shake of the head immediately disposed of it and sent it dangling down on its elastic under her chin, which was not the effect I was looking for. I tried again and again, with the same result, until I was forced to abandon the idea. I wanted Fenella to look cute, not drunk!

To match the tigress, I had made myself a brief green leotard, since the sight of a scantily dressed female never goes amiss in show business, and I, too, had a red ruffle to match Fenella's. Thus costumed, we were ready to venture into the great unknown, wondering how the public would take to our unusual, but well-loved pet.

Our act was in the first half of the show and followed a troupe of Arab tumblers. As the time for her first performance approached, I fastened Fenny's lead on her and led her along the wide passage. To reach the area outside the ring door entrance meant passing the tall, sliding doors behind which the elephant troupe was stabled. As if by magic, these doors, which had been wide open, quickly slid together. This happened every time we passed them, throughout the duration of the show. We never knew who caused them to be closed but always, as Fenny was led down the passage, the doors mysteriously closed.

Maybe the animal trainer presenting the elephants didn't like or trust tigers; maybe he thought that our tiger might attack his elephants, or that the latter, seeing an ancient enemy, might go berserk and run amok. It was obvious someone wasn't taking any chances.

The Arab tumblers were still performing, and the racing music which accompanied their act, together with their own shouts and yells, sounded very exciting. There could be no doubt that the sturdy man who bore the weight of the whole troupe was the strongest and mightiest man in the world. The acclaim of those he had supported voiced this fact to the whole assembly. The somersaults, leaps and spins, were greeted by those not performing with wild "Huzzas".

Waiting for them to finish was an ordeal, for Fenella, unlike a dog, would not sit on command; in fact, there was very little she would do on command. I had to walk her up and down the passage and round and round the area outside the ring doors, praying that she wouldn't become bored by the delay and decide it was time to lie down. If that happened, it would be a complete disaster, for often it took a long time to persuade her to get back on her feet. It would be a terrible anti-climax if, after the whirlwind finish of the Arabs, we had to go on and say, "There will be a short interval while we induce our tiger to come and show herself."

Then the Arabs, sweating and panting, came hurtling through the ring entrance to a tremendous roar of applause. Gone now was their vivacity, their shouts and beaming smiles. Like all acrobats, once they had finished their performance, they clung to any support that was to hand, sank into a couch, or flopped wearily onto the ground, whilst they paused until their exhausted bodies had recovered sufficiently to allow them to pick up their dressing gowns and seek the greater comfort of their dressing-rooms. They eyed Fenny warily and choosing a route as far away as possible from our tiger, they went their way.

Meantime a motley group of clowns were doing the things that clowns have always done, as the ring was prepared for our entrance. There were peals of laughter dying away as the clowns disappeared through the ring entrance.

At last it came, our announcement. The voice of Mr. Lockhart, the ringmaster, boomed over the loud speaker system: "And now, ladies and gentlemen, we have pleasure in introducing the Holmfirth Tiger." His voice rose to a crescendo as he pronounced the last words in great rolling syllables. The band struck up the strains of 'Tiger Rag': What else? - We were on!

Mercifully, Fenella stayed on her feet. The heavy, red plush curtains parted and my heart skipped several beats. This was far worse than anything I had done in the past, this voyage into the unknown.

I remember that entrance so vividly; what a long way it seemed from the ring entrance to the doors of the actual ring, and how slowly Fenny was walking. It was her usual gait, but in my excitement it seemed unusually slow, as though she was dawdling and taking all the time in the world. All my instincts as a performer told me we should make a bright and quick entry. I suppose I was never more keyed up in my life and I kept murmuring. "Please Fen, dear Fen. Don't sit down!"

To my relief she didn't, but plodded steadily on until she reached the brilliantly lit arena. A gasp of astonishment arose from the startled audience as Fenella, aware of what she had done earlier and with great presence of mind, stepped up on to the ring fence and continued on her graceful, sinuous perambulation. It was at this moment, I think, that I realised our pet - our Fenella - was indeed a born performer.

I didn't have to lead her, but just gently held the lead and walked by her shoulder - talking softly to her all the time, seeking to reassure her in what must surely have been very trying circumstances for her. Twice she stopped and looked around her, maybe disconcerted by what had happened to this place, previously bare and barren of people, now packed to the ceiling with buzzing humanity. Each time, after a momentary pause, she continued the walk on her own accord, with nothing more than a gentle vocal urging from myself. At long last we completed a full circle of the ring fence. I breathed a sigh of relief. All I had to do now was to wait for two or three youngsters to come and stroke her.

I heard a voice over the amplification system, familiar yet strange. I remember the shock when I realised that it was my father, because ordinarily he didn't sound like this at all, and he was asking if there was any child in the audience who would like to step into the ring and stroke Fenny.

We honestly thought we should be lucky to get more than one or two tentative offers from the bolder children, and certainly expected fond mothers to be reluctant to allow their offspring within biting and clawing range of the golden, striped creature in the ring who, everyone knew, could not be trusted for a minute.

For a moment there was a hushed silence, and I was sure that my worst fears were well founded. This was going to be an utter fiasco. Then, suddenly, the whole place erupted.

The Pied Piper of Hamelin could not have had a more astonishing effect. Every child in the audience seemed to bound out of its seat, surging, pushing and jostling its way to the aisles and pouring down them into the ring. Some children didn't bother to use the aisles but climbed over and under the seats in front.

Parents, usherettes, attendants, all sought in vain to stem the juvenile tide which flooded the ring. Soon they had completely filled the ring, the bigger and stronger fighting their way to the front. Fenny and I were surrounded by a load of exciting, chattering monkeys until we must have been utterly lost to the view of the audience. I grabbed Fenella's collar and held on to her as she weaved her way through and around a forest of legs, whilst sticky little hands stroked her fur and ran along her flanks. Maybe the audience saw an occasional wave of her tail, or a flash of her red collar, but whichever way she went, the surge of children went too. The youngsters were really enjoying themselves; so, too, was Fenella.

After what seemed an interminable time, order was eventually restored, and the children compelled to leave the ring. There, they stood, in a solid phalanx, unwilling to go back to their seats. Finally, we led Fenny away through the curtain.

I cannot even remember whether we received any applause after our exit, but I do know the feeling of relief I experienced when we were safely back behind the curtain, free of the maelstrom of excited children, none of whom had been nipped for their pains.

The management decided immediately that the red ruffle must go. "It makes her look far too tame," they said, and we agreed with them - even though we were, in fact, showing a tame tiger. I don't think that the Belle Vue management appreciated how really tame Fenella was, nor, for that matter, had we realised until then, just how much the tigress adored the whole human race, as opposed to individual humans whom she had always loved.

It was also decided that it would be better if, instead of inviting children from the audience and causing another invasion, I lead Fenny up and down the aisles, between the seats, so that those members of the audience near the aisle could reach over and stroke Fenny without leaving their seats.

The management was familiar with most types of wild animals, having a menagerie full of them, and, whilst they were aware that very friendly relationships can exist between keeper and caged animal, they could not credit an animal with Fenella's acceptance of human beings as friends and family. But if an accident occurred in the ring, the management would be responsible, and with so many children milling about, one of them might accidentally tread on the tiger's foot or tail and she, in anger, might injure one of them. It was a risk they couldn't take, so Fenny didn't wear her red ruffle any more. I, too, had a change of costume, for the girl assistants who had replaced the male ring hands now in the army, also wore red ruffles and clown hats similar to mine.

For the rest of our engagement at Belle Vue, I led Fenny up and down the aisles, murmuring the invitation, "Would you like to stroke her?" to anyone who seemed not too afraid of the tiger. Adults, who had read that tigers were extremely dangerous were more hesitant than juveniles, who saw Fenny quite clearly for what she was, an oversized, very beautiful and friendly pussy cat. The children, unless instructed otherwise by their parents, were always ready to stroke the tigress. Some of the young soldiers, however, preferred to stroke me!

On our return home from Belle Vue, we decided that a small transporter cage was needed, so that Fenny's slow and deliberate entrance, however graceful, could be speeded up. We could then rush her into the centre of the brightly lit auditorium and let the audience savour her beautiful, striped orange symmetry. A further thrill would be given when the door of her cage was suddenly opened and the tigress was let out. I would then lead her round the ring as I had done at Belle Vue.

By now we realised that, properly controlled, the unique position of possessing the only tiger in the world that any small child could safely stroke, was well worth exploiting. It seemed, however, better showmanship to keep Fenny in the centre of the ring, where the bright lights enhanced her beautifully marked flanks, and to allow a small section of the audience to come to us, than to take the tigress along the aisles. In any case, in the theatre, it would be virtually impossible to take the tigress out into the auditorium.

**Fenella being wheeled into the
circus tent in her transport cage**

Other dates followed. The government, anxious to maintain as high a morale as possible, advocated 'holidays at home' as most coastal holiday resorts of Britain faced the continent of Europe, from which now came the constant threat of invasion. The beaches of the south and east coasts bristled with barbed wire, sea defences, concrete pillboxes and the like, all set up to defy the enemy. Large stretches of the coast were prohibited areas and, in any case, low flying, marauding enemy aircraft were continually sweeping in over our shores to strafe and bomb anything that moved. It behoved people to stay at home, particularly in towns and cities far inland, where the enemy were likely to sustain great losses in trying to search them out. Many municipalities arranged open-air shows in their parks, and since Fenella was such an unusual attraction, requiring very little in the way of staging or properties to show her, we were in considerable demand.

Although these were dark days, life nevertheless went on. Everyone was working for the forces, essential services, or war industries. Money was plentiful, but things to buy were in great shortage. People worked long hours, for the factories continued day and night, every day of the year, so entertainment was eagerly sought. Cinemas were packed and the live theatre had a tremendous boom. Servicemen and women on leave had to be entertained and there was little thought for the morrow. The spirit of those days was, "Eat, drink and be merry, for tomorrow we die."

It was to the theatres that we took Fenella for the bulk of engagements. I suppose that most theatrical shows at that time were making money, but certainly the stage circuses were. There were so many restrictions on tenting shows in wartime that the circus virtually ceased to exist outside the theatres. So it was in the stage circus we slowly pieced together the performance we ultimately polished to perfection. We obtained a small cage, its four walls and roof all of gilt bars, which assembled neatly on to a platform standing on four rubber-tyred wheels. Into this, by either of the cage doors we had along each side, we could allow Fenella to enter. When 'her music' burst forth, and the announcement of her appearance boomed throughout the theatre, we would speed her into the centre stage.

My father, armed with a small hairbrush, then slipped into the wheeled cage with the tiger, having to kneel at her side as he brushed Fenella's flanks. The other door was opened and Fenny stepped off the cage. As she did so my mother slipped a noose of a whitened-braided cotton rope about the tiger's neck.

My mother, or I, led her round the ring, using the ring fence when it was wide enough, but often, on stage circuses, the front of the ring fence is disposed with, unless horses are in the ring. Sometimes the ring mat is taken away, and the acts perform on the normal boards of the stage.

An appeal for children to come forward to stroke the tiger was the signal for a host of children to rush from their seats, but it was possible, in the theatres, to prevent them from getting on to the stage. The disappointed children were directed back to their seats, whilst the lucky ones sat on the ring fence, or stood round the ring, whilst Fenny was led past them. After they had stroked the tiger, they returned to their seats, transported with delight.

Although Fenella must have been the world's most friendly tiger, she was still as unpredictable as other felines. Usually she could be cajoled and persuaded into doing the things we wanted, but there were occasions when she was not co-operative and could, in fact, be downright awkward.

This happened in Halifax, where we were touring with a stage circus. Only my mother and father were with Fenella, for by this time my sister and I had been conscripted into industry. Meg, although married, was working in a food shop and I had been directed into engineering, but as Halifax is only a few miles from home, Meg and I were able to see the performance at weekends.

Theatres, particularly the old provincial theatres, are nothing like the Hollywood versions. The dressing rooms are certainly not the palatial boudoirs shown in some films. They are usually grimy, cramped, with dingy greyish-blue or greyish-green walls, mottled mirrors, cigarette-charred dressing tables and naked light bulbs - or even empty sockets where the light bulb should be.

The theatre at Halifax was no exception. My parents' dressing room was beneath the stage and even smaller than usual. There was only room for Fenny's sleeping box, with barely room left to 'swing a mouse', much less the proverbial cat. The month was January. The weather was cold, damp and foggy. The mist drifted and swirled outside the theatre and seemed to be seeping inside it too.

Fenny was a creature who liked light and room to move about. The claustrophobic underground atmosphere seemed to have depressed her unbearably. My sister and I arrived that particular Saturday afternoon, after the matinee. The stage, which earlier had been ablaze of light and bustling with movement, was now silent and ghostly, ill-lit by small pilot lights. My mother was seated in the wings of the theatre beside Fenny's transporter cage, in which the tigress was lying disconsolately. Fenella had committed the cardinal sin of any performer: she had refused to go on!

As the week had progressed, Fenny had grown more and more depressed and had become increasingly unwilling to do anything at all. She had even become reluctant to leave the dressing room. The climax had come earlier that afternoon. Fenella, protesting strongly, ears flattened, lips curling in a subdued snarl, had eventually been persuaded to leave the dressing-room. Unwillingly, she had climbed the steps from the underground cell beneath the stage, and even more unwillingly had been persuaded to enter the transporter cage; when she was there, under a blaze of light in the centre of the stage, she had remained flat on the floor of the cage, ears back, eyes glinting wickedly and her tail twitching menacingly, as do all her species when they are annoyed.

Fenella had flatly refused to come out of the cage. So, faced with a problem they couldn't solve, my father had said - with some truth, I suppose - that Fenella wasn't well and her performance had to be abandoned. Since the matinee, my parents had not dared to take her back downstairs, and my mother had spent the intervening time sitting with the tigress in the wings, trying to win her back into good humour, obviously without success.

I bent down and put my head against the bars, as near to hers as possible. Fenny looked completely dejected.

"What's the matter, girl?" I whispered.

She lifted her head a little, gave a perfunctory chuckle - the whickering sound that tigers give as a form of affection - then resumed her glowering, sullen mien of utter dejection.

This was completely unlike her. Normally, she was a most affectionate animal. Even if she had not seen us for part of a day, she was usually overcome by emotion, snuffling, chuckling and rubbing against us. As a cub she used to collapse limp and helpless, against the object of her affection. Her recognition was, after the initial greeting, a complete and utter display of boredom. I might almost have been a stranger. "Better not catch her eye," my mother warned. "It only makes her snarl when she sees anyone looking at her."

We stood around, feeling utterly helpless and wondering what on earth we could do. We couldn't force her into action; to prod her and tease her in her present mood would only enrage her. It was one of the few occasions when the sheer ineffectuality of our position created a feeling of panic in all of us.

Fenella's name was blazoned in large lettering at the top of the theatre bills, proclaiming that she was a domesticated tigress, as tame as a household cat, a lover of humans and particularly of children, who could, quite safely, come on to the stage and stroke her. This moody, sullen, striped fury, lying angrily on the floor of the cage in no way resembled her billing.

The evening show was about to begin, and our tame tiger was still anything but tame. People were crowding into the theatre, having paid to see the tigress and it seemed more than probable that we should be unable to show her for the second time that day.

The other artistes were sympathetic and tried to be as helpful as possible, but they had far less knowledge of recalcitrant wild animals than we had.

"Perhaps she's got a belly-ache," said the man who presented the ponies. "Animals can't tell you when they feel ill."

The first act, a vaultage, with a rider leaping on and off his loping steed, had come and gone. Time was running out and we still hadn't persuaded Fenella to abandon her jaundiced view of life.

"If only we could get her to take an interest in something." said my father hopelessly, "If we could take her mind off her misery."

It was then that Meg showed a touch of genius. Her face brightened and she ecstatically mouthed one word, "Chips!"

"Chips?" I gasped, unable to follow the drift of her idea.

"Yes, chips" Meg explained. "Fenny hasn't tasted chips for ages and you know how she used to love them. Perhaps if we gave her some now, it would cure her."

Anything was better than just standing and looking forlornly at the tigress, although I had grave doubts of the success of Meg's idea. Quickly, we collected a torch from the dressing room and slipped out into the crow black night to look for a fish and chip shop. The mist, in chill wraiths, swirled about us in the almost deserted streets. Only an occasional car with dimmed headlights crept blindly through the fog-ridden night.

We hurried along, stumbling over a stone here, bumping into strange objects, as we turned down one cobbled street after another of that deserted Pennine town, sniffing the air like bloodhounds in search of the scent of that elusive fish and chip shop.

"There must be a fish and chip shop in a place as big as Halifax," complained my sister, but we were having little success in finding one. Suddenly, out of the grey-black fog, loomed a tall, male figure, hurrying towards us and clutching in his arms an untidy paper parcel. The smell was unmistakable. We were saved - oh surely, we were saved.

"Where's the fish and chip shop?" I blurted out after him, before he was swallowed up again in the fog. He stopped, peered owlishly through the fog, chewing some of his chips.

"Go down there," he said. "First turn left, left again, let me see, it's one, two, third door down."

Scarcely bothering to thank him, we dashed off into the fog, along the streets, then flicking on our torch and counting the doors. Could this be it? There was no sign of a shop from the outside. We opened the door and were faced by a heavy blackout curtain and beyond it there seemed a glimmer of light; the smell and hiss of frying fat was most noticeable. Breathing a sigh of relief, we pushed aside the curtain and there we were, in another world: There was blinding light, a glistening cooking range, and above all, the heavenly aroma of fish and chips.

"We'd better take enough," warned Meg, so I bought a whole shillingsworth, twelve times the normal amount, of smoking, hot chips. "No vinegar, please." I stopped the assistant just in time as she was about to splash my purchase with the contents of her vinegar bottle. With our precious parcel, tightly wrapped in newspaper, we hurried and stumbled back, in search of the theatre.

The interval was already over. There remained only fifteen minutes in which to work a miracle and arouse Fenny from her depressed torpor. Picking up a chip, my father slid it through the bars towards her nose. It was hot, fatty and luscious. We stood back in silence, hardly daring to breathe.

After a moment, Fenella's eyes opened wearily, her whiskers twitched slightly; she didn't lift her head, but her long pink tongue snaked out and carefully licked the chip. We all remained standing, pretending not to notice, but anxious to watch her reactions. She curled her tongue round the chip and it disappeared into her throat. She gulped - yes, she had swallowed the chip! Her pale nose dilated and she sniffed.

My father put a second chip close by her head, and again her tongue came out, swept up the chip, which followed the first down her throat. The next chip was placed just out of her reach, but sufficiently close for her to get the smell. If Fenny wanted this one, she would have to get up and collect it. Her gastric juices were slowly working and she was beginning to drool. We could hardly believe it - the tigress was sitting up and looking about her. She gulped the chip and was clearly looking for more.

We were terrified that she might change her mind and slump back on the floor, but no, she actually began to pace around in her transporter cage, and my father rewarded her by placing a few more chips inside the cage.

Suddenly the orchestra was playing our introductory music. We were on!

Quickly, my father stuffed a handful of greasy chips into the pocket of his smart, evening-dress jacket. "You'll ruin your suit!" My mother was shocked.

"What does it matter?" he replied. Hurriedly, he picked up the handle of the cage, with Fenella in it, and dragged it into the centre of the stage to start the show.

Fenella gave a remarkably good performance that evening, although it was somewhat unusual. Her exit from the cage was chip induced. She slobbered over chips as children from the audience stroked her back. She even chewed chips as the tigress wrestled with my father, the climax of our act. It was probably the stickiest, greasiest, wild animal performance in the history of the British theatre!

11

What, No Gun?

I have often been asked by incredulous people, "How did you manage to tame your tigress?" The answer was always the same, "Fenny was never wild."

Fenny's parents were wild animals, caged and suspicious, but she was taken immediately away from them and remembered absolutely nothing of them. Her parents, the ones responsible for feeding and tending her youthful needs, were human beings, by whom she had always been treated well, so her deep affection was for the humans who had replaced her natural mother.

"Fenny was never wild." I have always told my curious questioners." She has lived with us since the day she was born. She knows us and we understand her. She has her likes and dislikes, which we respect, but between us, we have a mutual trust in each other."

I must confess, however, that this is not quite so simple and straightforward as it sounds. Keeping a tiger as a pet isn't the glamorous business that you might suspect. It is a tiring and difficult job requiring constant vigilance. We could rarely go away together as one of the family had to stay at home to protect our pet to make sure she didn't get into mischief.

Meg's daughter Judy taking Fenella for a walk

This proved most demanding, but if one relaxed this watchfulness, it was possible that Fenella would quietly slip away into trouble. We weren't afraid of her savaging anyone or anything. We knew we could rely on her good behaviour, but there was no way of knowing how other people and animals would react to her, or what response that reaction would create in Fenny. These were the unknown factors against which we had always to guard.

She had once surprised me by jumping over the half-door of our caravan to chase hens and she could do the same again, after other prey. After years of ignoring the constant yapping of a neighbour's spaniel protesting loudly at the oversized cat walking in our garden, Fenella one day decided to inspect the nuisance who disturbed her afternoon rest. With one bound, she effortlessly cleared the intervening hedge and with the second leap captured the spaniel, whose yaps turned to terrified squeals as he found himself firmly imprisoned under the powerful front feet of the striped intruder. When the dog frantically squirmed to escape from its captor, it was natural for Fenella to use her claws to prevent the dog from escaping. This increased the animal's terror and caused slight laceration to its facial fur.

There were other times when she was incredibly calm and well-behaved. When she walked round freely amongst us, when she lay on the settee, elegantly washing her beautiful coat, or, asleep on her back - limp and vulnerable - in a foolishly endearing way, it didn't seem possible that we - ordinary people living in an ordinary house - could actually be living with a fully grown tigress.

Friends with preconceived notions about the treacherous nature of tigers were frequently worried about our safety. "Do you really mean that you haven't a gun? You must have some kind of defence," they insisted, "what if she turns nasty and attacks you?"

"Of course we haven't a gun," my father used to retort scornfully. "Why should we? Fenny is not ferocious. It is man who is a ferocious creature and expects all nature to emulate him. Man makes war on his own species and kills them off 'en masse'. My tiger never harmed anyone and has no desire to do so!"

As Fenella grew up, it became increasingly obvious that although she loved all the family, my father was the special favourite. Whenever he was absent for any length of time, the tigress used to sit, listening intently for the sound of his footsteps. Quickly, she learned to recognise the noise of the car outside the house, even seeming to know the notes of the engine. Before the car actually stopped and certainly before anyone else was aware that my father had returned, Fenella, alert, slid swiftly off her couch and stood expectantly behind the back door. As soon as my father entered the doorway, Fenella rose on her back legs, placing her heavy front paws on his shoulders. She would run her muzzle, with its stiff white whiskers and sloppy chops, endearingly against his cheek, to which he responded by speaking affectionately to her. Often their caress culminated in a playful roll on the floor as my father collapsed under the weight of our striped pet.

Neither my mother, my sister Meg, nor myself, merited so rapturous a reception. On many occasions, Fenny sniffed at us, rubbed her head against us, uttering her strange, chuckling sound of affection and was always happy to see us again and welcome us home. But the pleasure was never so ecstatic as when she greeted my father. Sometimes I used to suspect that Fenella realised that we, as females, were sisters under the skin and as such, could be ordered about, if she so wished, whereas my father was a man - a male who had to be greeted and obeyed.

Their playful rolling and wrestling was quite sensational, unprecedented between man and tiger, and was soon introduced into the act, adding more drama and excitement to it. At the same time, we began to use a large red and white striped, hessian ball, filled with fresh straw that made exciting noises as Fenny pounced on it. As the ball swung high above her, she executed spectacular leaps in her attempts to capture it, movements which were admired by an astounded audience.

For the wrestling scene, my father wore a succession of dinner jackets which disintegrated in rapid succession as they suffered rips and tears from the tigress's claws. He used to start the act well dressed in a smart dinner jacket, but when the wrestling scene was imminent, he slipped away to don one of the many old jackets, which would be further savaged as they rolled and wrestled in a circus ring or on a stage.

After each show, my mother patiently sewed the tears and rips, endeavoring to make the coat whole in time for the next performance, but invariably fighting a losing battle to preserve the tattered jackets.

As we travelled around the country we called at a succession of second-hand clothes dealers, searching for extra dinner jackets, all of which had seen better days, and all destined to be shredded by the tiger's sharp claws as she rolled and wrestled with her favourite human.

To try and preserve the hard-to-get clothing in those difficult days of rationing, we always endeavoured to keep the sharp points of Fenella's claws clipped, but this proved far from easy. Tigers' claws are composed of layers of very tough, horny material, and the curved point is extremely hard. Although clipping didn't hurt Fenny at all, it was similar to cutting a human toenail, the tiger objected to her claws being cut and was, I imagine, more than a little proud of them - neither did she like having her feet played with because, I think, she was ticklish in that area. I discovered that the best time to try to affect a manicure was late in the day, after she had eaten her supper, had washed herself and settled down for the night - but this would take a tediously long time. Just as it seemed Fenny had completed her toilet, she remembered some other part of her anatomy that merited another lick. It was all a most painstaking and leisurely business with Fenny, but hard on the long-suffering manicurist who had a host of other things to do.

Eventually, as Fenella began to doze, our strategy was to sit as close as possible beside her, softly whispering endearments and stroking her gently, to allay any suspicions she might entertain about our presence. Then Meg, or I, carefully explored her paws, searching for the sharpest claw and carefully easing it from its furry sheath. This done, another member of the family, standing close by with a pair of clippers, would deftly snip off the needle-sharp point. (Almost everything accomplished with Fenny was a double-handed effort, making looking after her so difficult.)

As soon as a sharp claw point had been removed, this almost invariably meant the end of the exercise for that day. Immediately, Fenella adopted an offended expression, as though we had betrayed her and the affection shown had been false, in order to rid her of one of her prize possessions. Her lips curled into a snarl, and she tucked her paws protectively underneath herself out of harm's way, very wary of any further intrusion on her person.

A repetition of the experiment immediately was unlikely to be successful, as Fenella remained suspicious and on her guard, and several days might pass before we were able to snip off another offending claw. As her claws grew at an alarming rate, our raids on them often resulted in failure.

In many ways, Fenny's conduct proved to be totally unlike the reputed behaviour of tigers. There is the theory that wild animals are terrified of fire and explorers in the jungle are frequently recorded as lighting fires at night to ward off wild animals. But Fenella never showed the slightest fear of fire. Instead she often padded across the hearth rug in front of our open coal fire, and then stopped to gaze speculatively at the dancing flames. Sometimes her waving tail became too close to the hot flames and was actually singed by them, but this never seemed to worry her. I must admit, however, that she rarely sprawled in front of the fire, nor basked in the warmth of its glowing embers, as a cat or dog will do. Fenella much preferred the elevated position offered by her special resting place on the front room settee.

There was another popular fallacy that was disproved by Fenella. How many times has it been quoted to us from so-called experts on wild animals, and from those whose knowledge came from books, but who had never kept one, "Ah, but if she ever smells human blood she will turn on you." This may be true of some wild animals, but if so, Fenny was the exception to the rule.

To test our tigress, I showed her a bleeding scratch on my finger. Fenella sniffed at it with polite interest, as this was expected of her, but immediately turned away to allow her mind to wander along the path it had previously been pursuing. Human blood obviously meant nothing to Fenella.

However there were some smells associated with human civilisation that had most peculiar effects upon her. Some perfumed toilet soaps almost sent her drooling with ecstasy. I have seen her lick a tablet of scented soap, then roll and squirm on the floor, in exactly the same manner as a dog when it discovers something which is, to humans, obnoxious and evil smelling.

I remember well a garrulous visitor, dressed in costly furs, who had travelled from a distance to see Fenella. Her hat, a mass of feathers, flowers and veiling, must have been the ultimate in the milliner's art, and was as expensive as the cloud of perfume that enveloped her. She was an obvious 'animal lover', and the sensuous, slinky grace of our tiger, and the exotic colouring of her striped coat, was something with which the lady easily identified herself, and found rapture in beholding.

"Oh, darling, " she exclaimed in loud, exultant tones, and deliriously stroked Fenny's shining ranks.

The admiration was not lost on Fenella, who had early learnt to recognise human sounds of admiration and affection. Their love affair was quite mutual, for the tiger was overjoyed by the expensive aroma which emanated from the silken-clad figure.

As a domestic cat rubs its flanks around the shins of a human friend, so Fenny rubbed her golden coat against the silken knees of this latest admirer.

"Oh, you darling," the lady gurgled again, and the lack of variety in her endearment was more than compensated by the intensity of her delight.

The lady then bent down and put her fashionably bedecked head closer to Fenella, who responded by thrusting her own giant head into the admirer's face, muzzling against her in delirious pleasure, breathing in the erotic perfumes that had been applied so liberally to her face and neck. Fenny's eyes had become glowing and bright, and I realised from the eagerness of her attitude that she was becoming too excited. I tried to divert her attention, but the allure of the perfume drew her like a magnet towards the visitor, who was quite unaware of the reason for the tiger's ecstatic fervour for her presence.

"She likes me, she likes me," trilled the lady happily, but suddenly, a note of alarm entered her voice at a completely unexpected (to her) change of circumstances.

Fenny, unable to restrain herself further, did what she often did to us, but what must have been most alarming to the fashionably dressed visitor. The tigress rose on to her back legs, wrapping her front paws round the visitor's neck and shoulders, effectively removing the decorated hat and sending the poor woman sprawling helplessly on the floor.

Quickly, we extricated our over-amorous pet and assisted the bewildered lady to her feet again. It seemed that a cloud had come over the beautiful friendship that had been so speedily created by this beautifully coiffured female human, and fanned to a fierce flame by the aura of Chanel No. 5. It was not quite the end of the affair, but certainly the honeymoon was abruptly terminated.

Different smells affected Fenny in different ways, and it often seemed that a lifelong reaction arose from her first introduction to a new aroma. If the tigress liked it, then her affection for the scent was constant, but if, for some strange reason, she took an instant dislike to a new scent, then not even the passage of years and subjection to the smell ever reconciled her to it.

There was the matter of my father's new slacks. We were showing Fenella at a Municipal Holidays at Home Gala, and a very fine marquee had been erected for the occasion. My father, in an effort to look as smart as the surroundings, was wearing a new pair of slacks as he led Fenny round the marquee. As far as we were aware, Fenella was familiar with serge, woollen, worsteds, and all the cloths from which male nether garments are manufactured, and the adoption of a new pair of slacks would normally go unnoticed. Not so on this occasion. Something about the cloth fascinated and repelled her, as a result of which, her behaviour became extraordinary.

Fenella persisted in wrapping her paws round my father's legs, grappling with him and tripping him up. In vain, my father tried to stop her; he tried pushing her away, admonishing her firmly, but all to no avail. Once Fenella got an idea in her head it took a great deal of moving, and it suddenly became clear to us that the material of my father's slacks must be responsible for this quite abnormal behaviour.

My father was in a most embarrassing position. Here he was, showing a reputedly tame and friendly tiger, who gave all the signs of wanting to chew his shinbone.

It was practically impossible to repel the constant attacks whilst still grasping the lead. To escape some of this unwelcome attention, my father hastily passed the lead to me which at least enabled him to remain clear of the now unfriendly animal. But even whilst being led by me, her attention was not diverted and she still tried to stalk my father's feet. Since Fenny was a heavy animal, I was afraid to tug too violently on her lead, and my father had continuously to step away, dancing quickly out of her reach, as Fenny determinedly pursued her efforts to come to grips with the offending legs.

Immediately my father changed back into his old pants, Fenella behaved perfectly. It was annoying in these days of clothes rationing to be unable to wear a new pair of slacks, but there was no other alternative. Fenny's strong objection to them inflamed her with the desire not only to be rid of the trousers, but also of the person who was wearing them.

Although the tigress had no 'doggy' smell about her, nor any perceptible odour - for she kept herself scrupulously clean and well-groomed - she did have certain animal characteristics. When ambling around the garden, she would, on infrequent occasions, when brushing against a bush or privet hedge, lift her tail and spray the leaves with urine. I don't know whether this was an inherent invitation to any male tiger, or it could have been a form of marking her territory, or, possibly, a reflex action which resulted from certain forms of contact. Whatever it was, it was something we never boasted about. My mother invariably reproached her sharply. "Fenella, lady tigers don't do that kind of thing, only tom cats." The reproof had no noticeable effect. Fenella only stared at my mother, eyeing her enigmatically, and then sniffed around the bushes she had so recently sprayed. Although seemingly intrigued, she usually wrinkled up her nose and pulled a face at her own scent.

In the garden, where the smell quickly vanished and the earth absorbed the urine, no harm was done, but it was a habit which, despite our supervision, Fenella occasionally indulged in whilst at some of the theatres we played. There were several sets of drapes and curtains that the tigress sought to identify as her own terrain by a quick squirt. After the show, when the building was quiet, I have often gone to try and sponge off the marks, hoping that the stage manager had not noticed our pet's scant treatment of his draperies.

I must confess, however, that many of the slinky theatre cats that inhabit backstage, were not oblivious to the strange smell. I have seen more than one sniff timidly at the sprayed site, then their hackles have risen and their hair stood on end as they inhaled this queer jungle smell. With their round eyes wide with scared astonishment, and their tails erect and stiff as flue brushes, they scuttled away to hide in some dark cranny.

My mother, whom Fate had destined to play the major role of attendant to our tame tigress, must occasionally have been in the line of fire as Fenny sprayed her new surroundings. As a result, she found herself in an embarrassing situation one day in the High Street of Rochdale. A mongrel dog passed close by my mother, and immediately became attracted by the scent which emanated from the hem of her coat. As he was a curious dog, and had little to do that day, he decided to investigate, and there was mother, walking about her business, with a mongrel passing beside her, sniffing the strange aroma she carried with her.

It was soon evident that the odour was not to the dog's liking, and even aroused dread and foreboding in the beast. Full of some instinctive fear, the dog bared its teeth, raised its hackles, and from its throat came a rumbling growl, deep at first but rising in intensity. Hastily, the mongrel backed away and started to bark in high-pitched protest. Passers-by looked in surprise at the inoffensive woman carrying a shopping bag, and being assailed by this frenzied animal who clearly found her presence so very disquieting.

My mother tried to ignore the dog. She walked as nonchalantly as possible, pretending the creature didn't exist, which wasn't easy considering the amount of protest being made. Without getting too close, the dog resolutely followed her from a safe distance, continuing to bark a warning to the world about this strange woman. Becoming desperate, my mother quickly went into the Post Office, hoping to deter the dog but in he came, through the open door, yapping frantically. Trying to shoo the dog only resulted in louder barking. It was only when she reached the safety of the stage door of the theatre, which she shut quickly after her, that my mother escaped from the demented animal.

Although most people were intrigued and somewhat surprised on first seeing Fenella, there were others who never accepted the tiger's liberty and regarded her freedom as a constant threat to their own. Travelling throughout the country and continually meeting new people, we encountered several amusing situations, although our hilarity was not always shared by the other participants.

One incident occurred when an animal trainer with his act joined the show in Cheshire. The trainer must have scanned the theatre and knew that he was sharing the bill with a tiger that week - but perhaps he imagined that it would be behind bars, a conventional caged animal.

Our more-than-dramatic meeting took place on the Monday evening as I was walking Fenny from the dressing room to the stage in readiness for her performance. Behind the stage was a corridor and as we strolled one way, the newcomer, with his ponies and dogs arrived from the opposite direction and we met face to face.

I shall never forget the look of horror and disbelief on his face. If the man could have turned and run he would have done so, but retreat was impossible. Behind him, blocking the corridor, were plump Shetland ponies whose bridles he held in one hand. In his other hand, were several leads attached to a troupe of frisking and assorted dogs. The trainer stopped, rooted in his tracks and his eyes boggled.

I stopped also, but Fenny, as was her habit, continued to walk and, fortunately, turned round in the opposite direction.

Freed from confrontation with the tiger, the man was galvanised into frantic action. He dragged bridles and leads and pulled his troupe forward to a door which entered the stage and forward into safety. The boards of the theatre rattled with the staccato hooves. His panic must have been complete, for I was just in time to see the door between the stage and the auditorium swing to behind him.

"Nay!" said the stage manager helplessly, for this was something outside his experience. Beyond the stage door the ponies' hooves were more muffled as they pranced up the aisle to the back of the theatre.

Cautiously, the stage manager opened the pass-door and peered out into the auditorium to watch the cavalcade of horses and hounds in the wake of their frightened trainer.

"Would you believe it?" he gasped in amazement. "The silly fool's taken the lot of them into the GENTS!"

For some time the trainer remained in the gents with his troupe of animals, but it was confidently expected that once he had overcome his initial fright, he would return to his proper place on the actors' side of the safety curtain. The show started and he was still secure in his rather unusual sanctum.

One or two patrons, desiring to use the facilities advertised, rattled in vain on the lavatory door only to find it bolted against them. As the time passed, the ringmaster showed signs of concern. "Go and tell him to come out immediately," he directed one of the stage hands, "and tell him that he's the next act on." The local worthy disappeared on his errand and soon returned.

"He says he's not coming out while that bloody tiger is about," was his message. Angrily, the ringmaster strode forward to reason with this awkward performer.

"It's all right," he hissed through a crack in the toilet door, for the show was now in full swing, and it was beginning to look as though off-stage events might prove more fascinating than the actual performance itself.

"The tiger is in its cage." reassured the ringmaster.

"Are you quite sure?" muttered the trainer, "I don't want any bloody tiger eating my animals."

Reluctantly, and still apprehensive, he was persuaded to lead his troupe back to the stage. But whilst he was performing on the stage with his animals, I had to drape Fenella's small transporter cage with covers and old blankets, so that neither he, nor his charges, could see the dreaded monster that lurked under the shrouds, ready and eager to tear his troupe to pieces.

A Strong Man was with the show for a few weeks, and whilst he seemed fascinated with Fenella, he had very little faith in her continuing tameness. According to his billing, he hailed from the Balkans, but as he spoke no English, the matter of his origin could never be pursued. Whereas the rest of the cast did not try to avoid the tigress when she was on her lead, the mid-European gentleman, for all his strength, was terrified of being on the stage at the same time as the tiger.

When the Strong Man arrived at the theatre, he timidly peered on to the stage, before coming any further. In his dressing room, he used to poke his head outside and look apprehensively along the corridor. If Fenella was in sight, he bolted back into the safety of his room. Whenever I took Fenella on the stage for exercise during the day, and if the Strong Man was in the theatre at that time, I would find him peering timidly from the safety of some remote doorway, apprehensive and yet enthralled by this creature the mad English family regarded as a pet.

In direct contrast to the man who locked himself and his animals in the gents, was a performer who had so little regard for the safety of his charges, that he even tethered his ponies to the bars of Fenella's cage. Their presence excited the tigress, and this habit was more than a little worrying. More than once, I had to untie his horses and tether them against some more permanent part of the theatre's structure, since it was practically impossible and fraught with hazard to take Fenella out of the cage when several ponies were fastened to it.

When I spoke to this trainer and asked him to discontinue using the cage as a tethering post, he replied abruptly, "What for? She's tame, isn't she?" It did not seem to occur to him that his charges might resent the paw of a tame tiger prodding their sleek round rumps.

However tame she was, Fenny always had a mind of her own, and whilst, generally, we could persuade her to do almost anything we wanted, there were occasions when it was necessary to compromise. Shortly after the winter season at Belle Vue circus, proved to be such a time.

Until then, although Fenella spent most of the day in our house in Yorkshire, whenever we were at home, each night she was taken to her quarters in the hut. This seemed a mutual arrangement; large dogs are in kennels each night and this seemed the proper treatment for our large cat.

When she was younger it would have been impossible to leave her in a room alone while in the house, because of the damage that she might do to furniture and upholstery, not willfully, of course, but with playful boisterousness. Now she no longer chewed cushions and pillows we were able to let her go upstairs again into the bedrooms where she liked to be. Fenella loved BEDS! Maybe she associated beds as the sleeping places of the humans she regarded as her parents, and felt they were places where she ought to lie too. Maybe she just liked the comfort of them. Whatever the reason, she loved to lie on beds.

After her supper in the kitchen, Fenella loved to sidle off upstairs and clamber on to a bed. There, she milled around, twisting and turning in search of the most comfortable spot, then slumped down as though weary. But first she had to wash her face and groom her whiskers before putting her head down and curling up in sleep. If tigers had been capable of purring, this was the time when Fenella would have purred most ecstatically.

Kassie's daughter Rosamund with Fenella in the back garden

Unfortunately, when we were ready for bed, we had to go upstairs, wake the sleeping tigress, bring her downstairs, then take her outside into the darkness of the night and the solitary confinement of her hut, where she had a very comfortable sleeping box.

It wasn't long before Fenny began to show signs of reluctance to abandon our comfortable bed. Eventually, the time came when we had no alternative other than to haul her off it. We had to grip her back legs and pull whilst Fenella, annoyed, dug in her claws and gripped the blankets in her fangs, all the time uttering fierce growls of protest. Each night it became increasingly difficult, and the treatment wasn't doing the bed covers any good at all.

The only solution was to ban Fenny from going upstairs after her supper so the door to the bedroom stairs was locked. But Fenella still didn't want to return to the hut and it became more and more obvious that her desire to remain in the house had become a strong determination on her part, to stay with the family, and almost a point blank refusal to leave us.

As the time to return to her hut approached, Fenella threw herself down on the kitchen hearthrug and glowered at us. For weeks, we played a type of waiting game, trying to enveigle her into coming out of the house into the garden. If she could be lured outside, then she would amiably accept the fact that she must go to sleep in the hut.

Curiosity was her undoing and our greatest weapon in tempting her into the garden. Fenella couldn't resist investigating strange noises, so, at first it wasn't too difficult to entice her away from the house. The sound of a tin being rattled would intrigue her; a bucket clanked along the asphalt path; the ringing of a steel spade on a stone or the scraping of feet in the passage alongside the house. Once the droning overhead of a squadron of bombers, hopefully our own, had a very good effect. Unfortunately this could not be repeated to order.

Originally, these outside noises were guaranteed to intrigue Fenny and bring her to the open door, but she usually took a long time before actually going outside. She would peep cautiously round the door, one paw raised delicately, ready to take the next hesitant step, but not quite abandoning her position inside the house.

Our tigress was no fool, and each night she became increasingly reluctant to fall for our stratagems. This often meant that we had to wait outside on chill and damp evenings, making a variety of odd noises and hoping that she would soon appear, whilst she lay comfortably on the hearth rug, resolutely ignoring our attempts until, by some stroke of genius, we thought of a new and unusual sound which brought her to her feet.

Eventually there came a time when it was almost impossible to deceive her. Fenny had learnt to identify all the sounds we could devise. She had begun to see through our bluff and even to suspect our motives. It seemed that her trust in the family might well suffer in these circumstances.

Fenella on the lawn

It was then that my father came to a decision.

"It's quite obvious we can't go on like this," he ruled, "Fenny has shown quite clearly that she doesn't like being on her own in the hut at night."

The next day a quantity of wood was ordered and a new sleeping box made. The kitchen was rearranged and the box installed in that room. The time for compromise was over. We had capitulated. On the other hand, as a result, our tiger was even more an essential member of the family.

Fenella on the Caravan Settee

12

On Tour

Some of my happiest recollections are of the carefree, nomadic life under the big top with tenting circuses. As one's childhood memories are of long hot summer days, so my thoughts of the circus conjure up pictures of dew-laden fields, sparkling in the sun, the fresh smell of green grass and the rattle of wind-blown canvas. But, of course, there were days of torrential rain too, when the sodden ground became a sea of oozing mud. It was in the circus that I heard for the first time the old adage, 'Devon, glorious Devon, where it rains six days out of seven.'

It is hard to say why life in a travelling circus is so enchanting. Perhaps it appeals to the gypsy existing in most of us and the escape from bustling, overcrowded streets and cities. Whatever the reason, it was a great joy to travel lazily from town to village setting up our tents for a day here, a day there, and occasionally enjoying the luxury of a whole week.

The tenting circus, with its big top, and surrounded by a cluster of wagons and caravans, is almost a community of its own, where the outside events of the world seem of little importance compared with the human dramas within it. Differences of opinion among the hot-blooded Mediterranean artistes were always noisier, fiercer and more vociferous than among the calmer English members, but soon all was forgotten and forgiven.

Although the life is hard, circus people rarely wish to change it and regard stage engagements or indoor circuses as a poor substitute for the real thing.

On tour, Fenella always lived in the caravan with the four of us. My father had rigged up a bed for her at one end of the van, and this had bars, behind which she could be closed in if necessary. This, our first caravan, was quite small, and in those days of spacious caravans, must have seemed congested, with Fenella occupying one end and the rest of us, the other. While my mother cooked at the stove along one wall, our tigress used to weave her way sinuously around us, brushing against one and then another and, very obviously enjoying the close proximity and intimacy of living with the family.

In retrospect, this was what Fenny had grown to accept. Her life commenced in the limited accommodation of a railway compartment in South Africa, and this close contact was accepted as her natural environment. Although the caravan was larger than the train compartment, so, too, was Fenella, but she was always cheerful and just as adaptable as other circus artistes.

Neither the bustle of circus life, nor the constant travelling perturbed our tigress, who actually seemed to enjoy the twice-daily performances in the ring.

As it was important to give her exercise during the day, we often lingered behind after the rest of the show had moved on to the next day's venue, especially if there was a large field nearby. Sometimes we pulled up alongside a wide grass verge or other suitable places. Fenny adored long grass, wet with dew, and used to crouch down, pretending to stalk us. Sometimes a person would pass by on the road and it was always amusing to note their violent reaction to the oddity of encountering a tiger on a lead.

On one occasion, an elderly farm worker on his cycle approached us from behind while we were parked in a lay-by. Fenny, on her lead, was enjoying the spring grass which came almost to her belly. The man, who was cycling slowly, had ample time to analyse the strange phenomenon ahead of him on the grass verge. As he drew near, he dismounted from his cycle and quickly wheeled it across to the far side of the road, where he deliberately transferred the bike to his left side, so it was between him and the striped creature on the verge. Resolutely, he marched past, eyes forward, never turning to look in our direction. As soon as he was ten yards or so ahead, he mounted the bike and rode off at full speed. I often wondered how he recounted this strange episode to his friends, or if he just pretended he had dreamt the whole occurrence.

Then there was the episode when we must have been close to a training camp for motorcycle dispatch riders. Fenny was, as usual, enjoying herself in the tall grasses at the road side, when first one, then another of these riders zoomed into earshot and raced past us down the road. I don't think any of the cyclists saw the tigress, but she certainly saw them. She was crouched low in the grass, her bright eyes glittering, and as the cyclists roared by, Fenny sprang up as quick as lightning to give chase. Fortunately, this was prevented as she was on her lead, but Fenny still had great fun, crouching down and pretending to chase after them, as they sped away into the distance.

Moving objects fascinated Fenella. Even distant aeroplanes attracted her, whilst a low-flying plane roaring across the sky was an especial delight. Trains particularly thrilled her, perhaps prompted by early memories of the first months of her life aboard them.

One day, whilst exercising Fenny in a circus field bordered by a railway embankment, a train suddenly roared across the edge of the field. Immediately, Fenella set off trying to chase it, dragging me along at the end of her rope, desperately struggling to hold back the excited tiger. The engine driver and his mate, seeing themselves chased from far below by a tiger, waved to us in high glee, and even blew a cheerful whistle. I suppose they felt quite safe in their train cabins, at that distance.

When the war ended in 1945, we had imagined that shortages and rationing would cease immediately and that butchers' meat would be available. Instead, to our consternation, the food situation seemed to be worse.

When playing theatres for a week or two, we managed to establish contacts, and to find horsemeat shops, but as itinerant travellers, moving on almost every day, we had no time to do this.

Fenella at the caravan door

Finding horsemeat shops, or even a respectable knacker's yard where we could get meat for our tiger, proved a great problem.

By this time, Fenella needed five to six pounds of meat a day, as well as a pint of milk at lunchtime, and more than once poor Fenny had to go supperless to bed. We consoled ourselves by remembering that zoo animals miss a feed once a week, and that they don't receive midday snacks, but when we saw how dejected our supperless pet looked, it was small consolation. My mother sometimes remarked sadly that she could understand how a woman without means would steal to get food for her starving children.

All we could do was to commiserate with poor Fenny as she walked moodily backwards and forwards, looking more and more miserable and waiting in vain for the supper that would not appear that evening. Even munching my own supper of plain bread and butter made me feel guilty, though I knew she would turn up her nose at it in disdain. I actually found physical difficulty in swallowing the food; it seemed so unjust that we were eating while she had to starve.

Once we tried whale meat, which we saw in one or two shops in towns through which we were travelling. It looked rather like cow or horsemeat, but was a much darker red, and I thought looked unpalatable. Fenella was 'choosy' about what she ate, so I had an unhappy premonition that our problem was not going to be solved. Yes, I was right. The tiger refused to have anything to do with the strange-looking meat. In some ways this was rather peculiar, as Fenny loved cod liver oil, but her partiality did not extend to the flesh of a whale.

In Scotland, where deer roamed the Highlands, we found a supply of venison. This was wonderfully off the ration and must be the Godsend we were looking for as, in the wild state, tigers killed and ate deer. Regrettably, no one had explained this to Fenella and, to our dismay, she refused even to touch the large haunch of venison we placed before her.

Occasionally fortune was more kind. Once, in the Rhondda, we were visited by a small dark, Celtic gentleman, on an even darker night, who whispered to my father in a mixture of Celtic and English, that he had heard of our dilemma, and in return for a small consideration he was prepared to help us. Rather apprehensively, my father went out into the blackness of the night, following the instructions whispered by our mysterious visitor, to a secret rendezvous.

There was a general sigh of relief when he returned, neither coshed nor robbed, but blessing the Welsh in general and that particular Celtic entrepreneur in particular, carrying a strangely-shaped parcel which contained a whole leg of lamb and no questions asked! I realised it was wrong to promote the black market, but at the time it didn't seem so, especially as Fenny enjoyed her supper so immensely that night.

Often, during those weeks, we went without our own meat, hoarding the precious meat coupons for emergencies, to prevent Fenny from starving. As we were then rationed to about one pound of stewing meat each, per week, and Fenny could consume six pounds without difficulty, it meant that a whole fortnight's ration barely provided more than one meal for her.

Fortunately, Fenny enjoyed tinned salmon, but this, alas, was in short supply too, and the contents of a tin hardly sustained a hungry tiger. Nevertheless we bought all the salmon we could obtain, putting it on one side to be preserved as iron rations. It was little more than a morsel for her, but it did give her a reason to wash herself as she lay on her bed prior to going to sleep. I hoped it assuaged her hunger pangs.

It was mainly during our earlier tenting shows that we evolved the complete act ultimately performed by Fenny. Tenting circuses were usually short of artistes, which meant that we were allowed more time in which to do our act and more freedom to vary it and life was more leisured than in the theatre when the show had to close at a certain time to allow the audience for the second house into the building. Sometimes amusing incidents occurred quite accidentally which were appreciated by the audience, and so afterwards they were deliberately included in our tenting routine. We followed the comedian's rule of thumb, 'if it gets a laugh, leave it in the act.'

The end of the act was dramatic with Fenella enthusiastically wrestling with my father in the centre of the ring. The tiger thought this was a wonderful game and was frequently reluctant to stop. To end the fight, my mother used to clink a saucer and jug containing evaporated milk, which Fenny loved, as a reminder to our 'cat' that more interesting matters were waiting for her. Almost invariably Fenny stopped wrestling at this signal, sprang to her feet and loped across to where the saucer was placed in full view of the audience. This, she eagerly lapped until the milk was finished, strengthening our claim that the tigress was only an oversized cat.

My father, who had also risen from the wrestling bout, used to stand astride Fenella as she lapped her milk, then, taking a handkerchief from his pocket, he wiped Fenella's whiskers, after which he entreated her to blow her nose. Fenny must have had a sense of humour, for often she snatched the handkerchief away from my father and held it between her teeth. Next, my father used to roll up his sleeve and place his arm between the shining white fangs of the tiger, thus proving that her teeth were real and not made of rubber, as had sometimes been suggested by sceptical onlookers.

Gasps of astonishment and alarm could be heard at this point of the act! To terminate, a few small children, their eyes bright with excitement, were given a ride on Fenny's back. Before they were returned to their seats, my father used to say gravely: "When you grow up and tell your grandchildren that you rode on a real live tiger, they'll never believe you."

One of the industries which reopened after the war was caravan building, and at last we were able to order a larger caravan than the pre-war, cramped model we had used for Fenella and ourselves. We were quite convinced that this would be the answer to our problems. Fenella did not object to the overcrowding and seemed to enjoy the intimacy, but three adults and a fully-grown tigress squeezed into a small caravan presented many difficulties. It was decided, after a family consultation, that Fenella should have the small caravan all to herself as it had its built-in caged compartment at one end and she would have the rest of the space in which to parade. It seemed an ideal solution.

The idea of separate caravans, brilliantly conceived, we thought, did not - like many other brainwaves - work well. It was fine for us - we had the space for cooking and sleeping in comfort - but our tiger didn't like it at all. She couldn't understand why she was left on her own. Fenella was not an animal who liked privacy; nearly all her life she had been in close contact with the family and that was the way she wanted it to continue.

As a cub, when left alone, she had displayed a tendency to howl, and Fenny had not lost this capacity, nor acquired a more independent point of view. As an adult, she had a particularly melancholy cry, which started on a high note, extremely plaintive, then tapered off into a deep bass note, somewhat akin to the cry of a lowing cow. Apart from being most distressing to hear, it showed us quite emphatically, that our beloved tiger was feeling very lonely and miserable.

Fenella & Judith Antell, daughter of a friend,
outside the theatre at Reading

The only way to prevent this pitiful noise was to keep her company, and it became necessary to spend practically the whole day with Fenny. We began again to have our meals whilst we were with her, and soon we had almost moved back into the old caravan. It was ironic. There we had a splendid new caravan, spacious and comfortable, and we were forced to revert to our previous custom of sharing a much smaller, more confined and much less desirable caravan. The new one was so fully equipped that it was impossible to alter it when on tour and the whole summer season was passed in this crazy fashion.

When winter came, my father had the time to convert the new caravan to include Fenella and also to provide more space for us. A bed was ripped out at one end to be replaced by a compartment for Fenella. This was a great improvement.

Finally my father decided upon yet another addition to give Fenella more room to walk. It was her incessant stalking to and fro in the middle of the night that was often the most aggravating part of living with her. Like wild tigers in cages, Fenella always walked the fullest extent of the living space in her quest for exercise, and this included all our beds. Without scruple, Fenella included the beds in her perambulations and never worried about the difficulties in climbing on, or over, the recumbent bodies lying in the beds. For those seeking sleep under the blankets it was a trying situation. Sometimes I felt that Fenny deliberately walked over us with an idea that if she was awake, then everyone else should be too, although I often noticed that after we had reluctantly got up, ideas of any more sleep having vanished, the tiger, with a satisfied grunt, flopped down on to the vacated bed and made herself really comfortable.

The addition to the caravan was an extension along its outside, in the form of a verandah about four feet wide. It hooked on to the caravan on one side, was supported by legs at the front, and was surrounded by a fence of chain-link netting.

To our relief, Fenella accepted the platform and fence alongside the caravan as an extension of her territory, giving her additional space in which to exercise. As it was in the open air, there was also more to interest her than passing ceaselessly round the confines of the caravan. There was a gate to the verandah which had to be kept closed at all times.

It was an ingenious arrangement and a great success. Fenella could wander on the verandah outside while we completed our household chores, cooked meals, or just rested after travelling and making arrangements for the show.

I am not sure whether tigers are, by nature, principally nocturnal animals. Certainly Fenny never had any difficulty in seeing in the dark and could always find her way, however black the night. She also awoke extremely early in the morning and immediately started her daily exercise, padding silently about the van. In the small area of the caravan, a large animal like Fenella could and did sway the structure and caused a continued vibration which was most disturbing to would-be sleepers. When particularly tired, the constant shaking proved even more irritating, and certainly did not improve our tempers.

One early morning, my mother could no longer stand a heavy tiger walking over her. Surely this was the time to use the verandah. Half asleep, she staggered out of bed and opened the caravan door. "Out, cat," she hissed, and the object of her spleen happily slipped like an eel through the narrow aperture of the partially opened door, to disappear on to the verandah. Thankfully my mother flopped back into bed and turned over to seek blissful sleep.

But she didn't sleep for long. Some sixth sense warned her that something was amiss. There was absolute silence from outside where she expected to hear the padding of soft feet on the bare wooden boards. Nor was the caravan swaying as it should have been doing with a large animal promenading alongside it.

In a panic, mother shot out of bed, opened the door for the second time and peered out into the half-light of the coming dawn. There was no sign of the tiger and, worse still, the gate that should have been secured, swung gently on its hinges!

How long had Fenny been away? Could she have been asleep since Fenny was released on to the verandah? These questions assailed my mother as, hastily, without stopping to put on a coat, she leaped from the verandah onto the chilly, dew-laden grass.

There was nothing stirring, but from the direction of the horse tent came a little whicker, followed by a gentle snorting noise. Mother's heart thudded. Supposing Fenny had heard a similar sound, would she have headed in that direction? Worse still, was she already there? My mother ran headlong into the horse tent.

Inside, it was much darker, but two ponies turned to look at her through half-closed eyes. That was a good sign, because if Fenella had been there, they would surely have sensed her presence and registered more alarm than they were currently demonstrating. She was obviously not there, but where on earth could she be?

Mother tried to quell the terrible feeling of panic inside her and hurriedly walked round the vans, calling clearly but softly, "Fenny, Fenny." She peered about the caravans, under lorries and continued her frantic call without result.

Suddenly, the top half of a caravan door opened and the circus proprietor peered out with bleary eyes. "God, I thought you were a ghost!" he greeted her.

"It's Fenny. She's gone and I can't find her anywhere."

"Half a minute," he looked alarmed and shortly emerged huddled in an old army greatcoat. Following him was his wife, her hair in curlers and her face pale with sleep. "Here, love, put this on. You'll catch your death." She offered my mother, shivering in the cold morning air, a scarlet quilted dressing gown.

Together, Mother and the circus owner toured the site, peering under the vans and returning inevitably to the animal tents, as they were all that remained of the show, everything else being packed on to wagons ready to leave that morning. The owner gingerly peered behind some bales of straw and then prodded a small mound of hay, which seemed rather senseless, as it was hardly big enough to conceal a cat, much less a fully-grown tiger.

"It's no good," said my mother tearfully. "I'll have to go and tell him Fenny's gone."

In great distress, Mother turned to the caravan. She mounted on to the verandah, through the still swinging gate, and into the caravan, the door of which, in her haste and panic, she had left wide open.

"Wilfrid!" she blurted out, then stopped, taken aback, for my father was still blissfully huddled in the blankets, fast asleep. Beside him, lying at the top of the covers and regarding Mother with benign amber eyes, was the tiger she had searched for with increasing concern.

She sat down and cried.

Fenella, 10 years old with Rosamund

13

The Curtain Falls

Early in the year 1950, we joined a travelling variety show which was booked to play in some of the best variety theatres in Britain. Its title, 'Would you believe it?' was borrowed from a then popular strip cartoon, whilst the show consisted of strange or unusual acts that the general public would not credit were possible. It was presented by a compère dressed in the style of that master showman, Phineas T. Barnum.

I suppose a tiger which allowed children to stroke and play with it would have appealed to the famous Mr. Barnum, but I am not so sure about one of the acts on the bill, where a man swallowed the entire contents of a goldfish bowl in which swam a variety of marine creatures. He then regurgitated them back into the bowl, the fish swimming as gaily as before.

It always astounded me that the audience roared with laughter at the feat. To me it was utterly revolting.

This well-presented show had great prestige value and was an obvious attraction wherever it went. It was a pleasure to have comfortable, lavishly-decorated dressing-rooms, and an agreeable change from some of the dreary rooms we had occupied in less prosperous theatres. There was one unfortunate drawback; the theatre management were not prepared to allow Fenny to remain on their premises outside performing hours. This meant that we had to take her to and from the parking ground where the caravan was sited on dark, damp nights after the show was over.

The weather throughout the tour which had started in the south of England, had been extremely cold, and as we travelled northwards, each day became chillier. Travelling became difficult as often the caravan was buffeted by snowstorms and rain.

Eventually the show arrived in Sunderland, and it was there that Fenny, who had always been extremely healthy, became ill. This was a new circumstance and one which was completely outside our experience. At first we were not unduly worried and thought she must have caught a cold in the bitter north-east winds of Sunderland, winds that cut through you like a knife.

Her condition did not improve and each day she seemed worse, becoming more tired and listless. When she began to refuse her food we realised that there was something radically wrong and an uneasy feeling of fear and helplessness entered our minds. We were all relieved when my father decided that we should take Fenny back to the warmth and comfort of home in Yorkshire, for a caravan during that bitter, wintry period seemed no place in which to care for a sick animal.

We raced down the Great North Road, ignoring the twenty miles per hour speed limit imposed on goods vehicles with trailers in force at that time, stopping briefly at one place to request a can of water from a farm, for by then Fenny had developed a raging and insatiable thirst.

As soon as we arrived back at home, we installed her in the straw-filled box in the kitchen and lit a good, big coal fire, hoping desperately that the familiar surroundings, the warmth and comfort of her box, would affect an improvement to her pathetic condition.

The local vet was called in. He must have sensed the urgency of the call and arrived promptly. I don't know what his experience of tigers was, or whether he had any initial misgivings about entering a tiger's lair, but if he had any such misgivings they were quickly overcome by the immediate realisation that he was dealing with a very sick animal who had little interest in his presence.

His examination was not prolonged and his swift diagnosis was frightening.

"Nephritis." he said gravely.

We had no idea what that was, but it sounded most serious. "Meat-eating animals do tend to have it," he explained, adding, "It's a kidney complaint."

He didn't sound hopeful of the outcome. Before he left he administered an injection, but it didn't help.

Poor Fenella, she lingered on for a few more days, and to us, who loved her so dearly, it was agonising to see her beautiful face looking so drawn and her normally bright eyes chill and listless.

At the end, I was sitting beside her on the thick bedding of straw, my fingers gently caressing her noble brow, our darling Fenella passed into a coma and then, inevitably, the life drained from her.

It was night; the time she would normally have been rousing to give her show. She was ten and a half years old, a most gracious animal, and the only known tigress to spend her entire life with a human family.

We were all terribly distressed by her death. It was as though we had lost a very close and dear relative, for indeed she had always been a very special member of the family. The ten and a half years in her company had been constantly shared with her. Our entire life during that period had been geared to catering for her needs, to tending her, feeding her, and giving her perpetual companionship.

Suddenly there was no need for anyone to be continually with the tiger. The fact that we could all go out together again brought us no joy. There was a strange, lonely feeling, and a terrible blank in our lives; we felt her loss very keenly. Our reward had been that she regarded herself as one of the family; she had always been good-natured, friendly, and in her own way, extremely affectionate. Felines are by nature rather aloof and do not demonstrate pleasure as obviously as dogs, but to those who can understand the signs and sounds of a tiger, there is no doubt that Fenella was extremely happy and content living the life she did. Nothing had happened in her lifetime to make her alter her high regard for the human beings who had adopted her in early infancy and who she had always believed were her parents.

We buried her sorrowfully, with solemnity and more than a little reverence, in the large rambling grounds surrounding the house of a relation where Fenella had frequently played, stalking imaginary prey and wandering happily through the thick foliage. It was an appropriate last resting place.

Her death was reported in many newspapers, for Fenella had, in her time as the 'Holmfirth Tiger', been a famous celebrity. Stories were retold more truthfully than some of the war-time accounts, of how she was led through the country lanes, how she was patted and stroked by schoolchildren, and how she had remained, throughout her life, as docile as when she first came to Holmfirth as a half-grown cub in 1940. Her docility was far more apparent in later years. When she was younger, full of energy and exuberance, she had sometimes proved quite a handful.

Many people, remembering her glorious markings, expressed wonder that we did not retain her pelt as a tiger-skin rug. Indeed, she would have made a wonderful hearthrug. My terse answer was always the same, "Would you have your sister skinned and her pelt laid out as a rug?" The idea was unthinkable then as it is unthinkable now.

Even now, after twenty-six years, the legend of the 'Holmfirth Tiger' still lives on and stories of her prowess still appear in print.

Life is full of coincidences and when my daughter grew up she was attracted for a time to a career on the stage, becoming assistant stage manager and bit-player at Whitby for a summer season. In the company was an actress called 'Fenella' and my daughter, who was curious, asked her how she came to have that name.

"You'll never believe this," answered the young actress. "My mother once went to a circus and stroked a tiger named Fenella, she fell in love with the tiger and christened me with its name!"

It's a small and extremely interesting world.

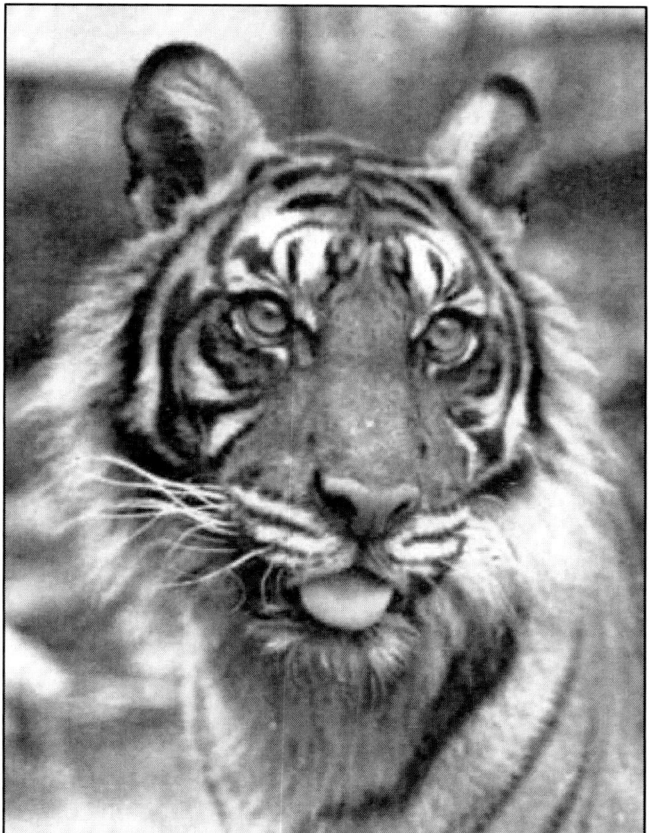